The Voyage of the *Argo*

Books by David R. Slavitt

POETRY

PS3569.L3
Epic and Epigram: Two Elizabethan Entertainments
A Gift
Crossroads
Eight Longer Poems
Equinox
The Walls of Thebes
Big Nose
Dozens
Rounding the Horn
Vital Signs: New and Selected Poems
Child's Play
Day Sailing
The Carnivore
Suits for the Dead

TRANSLATIONS

João Pinto Delgado's The Poem of Queen Esther
Three Amusements of Ausonius
The Persians of Aeschylus
Celebrating Ladies: The Thesmophoriazusae of Aristophanes
Epinician Odes and Dithyrambs of Bacchylides
Broken Columns: Two Roman Epic Fragments (Statius and Claudian)
A Crown for the King by Solomon Ibn Gabirol
The Oresteia of Aeschylus
Sixty-one Psalms of David
Hymns of Prudentius
The Metamorphoses of Ovid
The Fables of Avianus
Seneca: Five Tragedies
Ovid's Poetry of Exile
The Tristia of Ovid
The Elegies to Delia of Albius Tibullus
The Eclogues and the Georgics of Virgil

The Voyage of the *Argo*

The *Argonautica* of
Gaius Valerius Flaccus

TRANSLATED BY
David R. Slavitt

The Johns Hopkins University Press
BALTIMORE AND LONDON

The Johns Hopkins University Press
2715 North Charles Street
Baltimore, Maryland 21218-4363
www.press.jhu.edu

Library of Congress Cataloging-in-Publication Data will be found at the end of this book.
A catalog record for this book is available from the British Library.

ISBN 0-8018-6177-2
ISBN 0-8018-6178-0 (pbk.)

For Neil Welliver

Contents

Translator's Introduction

ALMOST NOTHING is known about Gaius Valerius Flaccus except that he was *quindecimvir sacris faciundis,* which is to say that he was a member of that group in charge of the Sibylline books and the supervision of foreign cults. He began his poem—his only surviving work—around A.D. 80, and he died before he completed it, probably in 92 or 93 (Quintilian expresses regret at his demise). His epic was discovered in 1416 at St. Gall in Switzerland by Poggio Bracciolini, but that manuscript has since been lost. Received wisdom from the classicists is pretty much what one might expect: they see the influence of Virgil (of course), discern similarities to Ovid, who preceded him only by a couple of generations, and point out the possibility that he may in turn have influenced the work of Statius and Silius.

That's it. That's absolutely everything there is to know about Valerius Flaccus except that his poem is not a slavish imitation of the better-known work on the same subject by Apollonius of Rhodes. I am content to let my rendition into English speak for Valerius, but for those whom I imagine standing in an aisle of a library or bookstore, trying to decide, I can offer some reassurance. This piece is playful, unpredictable, oddly contrarian, sometimes almost mannerist. Valerius' description in book 8 of Medea's putting the serpent to sleep so Jason can filch the fleece involves a gesture no other Latin poet I know would have thought to try—a brief moment in Medea's head when she allows herself to feel sorry for the snake:

> Medea, seeing it helpless, ran to it, weeping tears
> for pity's sake and in shame for her own cruel behavior.
> "Never once, in the darkest night," she exclaimed, "did I see you
> asleep at your post like this, when I brought you the honey-cake supper

you nibbled out of my hand. You great, poor, hulking brute!
What can I say? This way, I didn't need to kill you.
But when you wake, you'll look at your tree and see that the fleece
is gone and slink away to spend your old age in another
and, I hope, a better grove. Forget about me. Forgive me.
And do not come hissing and spitting to follow where I have gone."

It is this kind of droll surprise that drew me to undertake the translation of a work that is not, I freely confess, well known. The *Aeneid* and the *Metamorphoses* are standard texts in classics courses, but the rich and varied tradition of the Roman epic is terra incognita to most undergraduates and, indeed, to most lay readers. Some of these works are long and less than immediately appealing. Silius' *Punica* and Statius' *Thebiad* are unlikely to show up as selections of Oprah's Book Club, but Lord Byron thought Lucan's *Pharsalia* insufficiently appreciated and called it "an epic poem of great merit which read on classic ground is by no means uninteresting."

Even allowing for the litotes, any recommendation from Lord Byron is worth attention. And my guess is that, even with all the tens of thousands of college students arduously voyaging toward the sheepskin that is their goal, there are fewer readers of Roman epic now than there were in Byron's time.

I had done a little Statius and a little Claudian. Why not Valerius' *Argonautica?* Elaine Fantham was kind enough to suggest that I take a look at it. I did, was grateful, and am happy now to invite others to do so.

The Voyage of the *Argo*

Book I

Those straits the mighty sons of the gods first sailed, we sing,
and their sacred ship that dared the banks of Scythia's Phasis,
braving Symplegades' rocks that clashed together, and sank
and settled to rest at last in the depths of the starry sky.
Guide me, Phoebus, if ever a priestess in your shrine
on the tripod seat spoke truth, or if ever your laurel chaplet
graced a worthy head! And you, great pioneer
who breached the Caledonian seas you claimed as ours,
Vespasian, gracious lord, raise me up as I raise
my voice, and favor with your attention my reverent hymn   10
of the deeds of heroes of old. Your son Domitian sings
in pride of his brother Titus' martial exploits, his arms
covered in glory that shines through the dust of Jerusalem's ruin.
They both honor your line, as the temple he has erected
does you credit. Among our constellations, you
are the Cynosura helmsmen of Tyrian vessels seek out
in the Little Bear, or the Helice by which Greeks plot their courses.
As all the ships in the busy sea lanes from Sidon to Egypt
that venture forth must look to you for their safe passage,
so I invoke your aid for my voice to resound worldwide.   20
Pelias was old, that feared and powerful king
who had long ruled Haemonia's uplands, the mountains of Othrys,
Haemus, and lofty Olympus, from which the rivers descend
to the teeming Ionian Sea. But his mind was never at rest.
Dread dogged his every sleeping and waking hour,
and menace everywhere lurked, the threat of the hostile heavens,

the prophets long ago having declared that the king
would be destroyed by his brother's house; instead of love
and honor, ruin waited, the blood blood-kin would shed.
30   These dire omens repeated their grim message from altar
to altar, the victims' vitals menacing and malformed.
To whom should the king then look, not with an uncle's pride
but half-crazed with fear and suspicion of that great hero?
Jason, Aeson's son! These were times of peace
and he could not send him away to fight somewhere. What monsters
were left to challenge? Hercules, long ago, had subdued
the Nemean lion and hung on the temple walls its jaw.
The countryside was safe from the dread hydra of Lerna
dispatched along with the Cretan bull and the Minotaur.
40   In the absence of such fierce creatures of supernature,
the sea still seethed in its might, a danger quite sufficient
for Pelias' purpose. With looks of love and concern, he addressed
his nephew Jason and gravely spoke his deceitful words:
"Do me this service I ask — and offer: a valiant deed,
an undertaking to rival those exploits of long ago
of which we speak even now in reverence. You know the legends
of what our kinsmen did and suffered, the tale of Phrixus,
Nephele's son, who fled our hearth and household altars
to roam the distant roads of the earth, and traveled even
50   to the icebound Phasis River in Scythia's plain. There
the savage king Aeëtes, in arrogant desecration
of the laws of host and guest and the banquet table's decorum,
slew him — a horror to make the Sun avert his face.
This is no mere story, but happens before my eyes
every night when they close at last in exhaustion: I yield
to the dream that stains my repose. I see him die, and his sister
Helle, who went there with him, mangled and drowned in the sea.
It rankles that I am old and have lost the strength of my limbs
with which I should extort from the land of Colchis the heavy
60   penalty transgressions of such monstrosity merit:
the arms of that king, or better his arms and his bloody head . . .
But I bear the weight of my years. My blood runs sluggish and cold,
and my son is a stripling, not yet ready for battlefields
or the seafarer's trial by water. I turn to you, my nephew,

kinsman, and friend, whose strength may salvage our wounded pride.
Go there! Bring back the golden fleece of Nephele's ram
and restore that sacred relic of Greece to its rightful place
here in our temple. You have the requisite strength and courage
for the undertaking of such a noble and perilous task."
With such artfully chosen words did the old king urge,   70
or one might say command, the young hero. The snares
that lay in the way, the dreadful floating islands that crash
together to stave in the hulls of the brave or very foolish
who venture into the Black Sea, he neglected to mention.
To the fearsome dragon that guarded the tree on which the fleece
was hung in the branches, that hissed and flicked out its forked tongue,
that beast the barbarous princess had conjured with magic charms
and honey-cakes prepared with deadly exotic toxins,
the ruler failed to make even a passing reference.

    Jason is not stupid: he understands how the king,   80
indifferent to any sheepskin, is driven rather by hate
and expects the expedition to end in ruin and death.
Why should he accept this impossible mission to Colchis?
Even if he could fly with Perseus' wingèd sandals
or ride in Triptolemus' chariot dragons draw through the skies,
the adventure would still be all but impossibly daunting. And yet
what other choice remains? To stir up fickle subjects
and fan their discontent with their old peremptory ruler
into the flames of rebellion? Such a thing is distasteful
even to contemplate. Rather, he will rely   90
on Juno's help and that of Minerva, shining in armor.
He will do as the king has charged him, but perhaps with better result
if the sea allows his crossing. Success against all odds
and therefore even renown could be his reward. Glory!
Your fire warms men's souls as it quickens their hearts and minds.
He can see your beckoning figure ghostly there in the distant
mists of the Phasis Valley and hear that siren's song
that inspires men to try their mettle. Are they heroes
or mere dreamers? Jason prays to heaven for strength
in the first crucial contest—against his own self-doubt.   100
He raises his hands to the skies in which he will put his trust
and prays: "O Queen of Heaven, remember me! When mighty

Jove darkened the skies and rain sluiced down to soak
the earth and craze the trickling streams to savage torrents,
I carried a woman once on my shoulders to help her cross
the turbulent Enipeus. She rode across dry-shod
and then, at the farther shore, at a thunderclap she vanished —
called perhaps by her husband home to heaven. Frightened,
I knew then who you were. I call on you now, O Queen,
110   for you were she, and mine was the honor of that good deed.
Grant that I may arrive at Scythia where the Phasis
pours into the sea. And you, Pallas, protect me
and keep me from harm's way. Then will I offer that fleece
as a gift to deck your shrine, and my father, relieved and grateful,
will dedicate sacrificial victims, cattle with gilded
horns picked from his snow-white herds he'll lead to your altars."

    The goddesses hear and are moved, and swiftly fly through the air
in different directions. Minerva heads to Thespia first,
alighting there to bid King Argus fashion a vessel
120   from massive timbers felled and hewn with his own axe,
and she goes with him to the shady groves on Pelion's foothills.
Juno, meanwhile, visits the various cities of Argos
and Macedon to proclaim how Aeson's son will adventure,
trying the winds and waves as no man has before him.
The ship they now are building needs oarsmen of strength and daring.
To such, she offers protection and the prospect of exaltation
that mortals may on occasion earn by their glorious deeds.

    Inspired, men of repute in seamanship and warfare
are eager to undertake the perilous expedition,
130   as those in their first flower of manhood rejoice at the chance
to see for themselves if their dreams of valor may now come true.
Complacent farmers and ploughmen, who delight in the fauns of the wood
and the gentle play of the woodland and river nymphs, sing praises
of the ship of which they have heard with its crew of assembling heroes.

    First, of course, from Tiryns, Hercules hurries, he
with the arrows dipped in poison and the bow his companion Hylas
carries across his shoulders. (His hands cannot encircle
the grip of the huge club.) Juno is furious, frenzied
seeing that pair, and complains, "Of all the young men of Greece,
140   why him, whom I hate but now must help to prosper?

Jason has asked my aid, and I cannot impede their progress
by means of my husband's storms, but I hate to accept his help
and count on him as one of the *Argo*'s shipmates to whom
I shall be forced to acknowledge a debt of my gratitude."

  She spoke and turned her eyes to the work of the busy shipwrights
sawing the axe-felled pine into the pliant planks
they steam over their fires to the curvature of strakes
for the great ship. Others are fashioning oars and spars,
and Minerva herself is searching the tall trunk that will serve
as mast for the square sail. A solid vessel, it stands   150
at the shore of the sea whose rage will test its strength and worth.
When the workers have daubed the joints with sealing wax, King Argus
paints on the sides of the prow the icons to grace its voyage.
On one side, Thetis, the nymph the greatest of gods had wooed,
is borne on the back of a dolphin to Peleus' bedchamber;
the dolphin cleaves the waves and her face is veiled as she rides him,
but one may suppose her expression is rueful—the son she will bear
the Fates have said will exceed his sire, and therefore Jove
has renounced her, giving her over to Peleus, a mortal.
The nymphs Panope and Doto and Galatea are swimming   160
alongside her, escorts, as she makes for her honeymoon cavern.
From a bluff on the shore the Cyclops calls out to Galatea.
Matching this is a fire and a seaweed banquette where Phocus
feasts with his wife Psamathe, while Chiron strums his lyre.
On the other side of the prow are Pholoë and Rhoetus,
maddened with wine, and the famous fight of the centaurs and Lapiths,
bowls and pitchers flying, and chairs and tables, too.
Among the brawlers appears the face of Peleus, spearman
par excellence, and near him Aeson, hacking his way
with his broad sword. Monychus struggles in vain with Nestor,   170
who rides astride his back; Clanis is holding a blazing
tree trunk and killing Actor, while Nessus, the centaur, flees,
and Hippasus sprawls on the floor with his head in a golden goblet.

  Jason pays little heed to these representations. His father's
likeness adds to his burden. "Alas for fathers and sons!"
the hero broods, "for under a threatening sky, we embark
for the sake of a hostile king to confront a turbulent sea
and wild winds in a fragile vessel. But what shall I do?

Shall I enlist Acastus, Pelias' darling son,
180 as shipmate, companion, and also hostage? Then would the father
join in our mothers' fervent prayers for our safe return."

   As this thought crosses his mind, an eagle crosses the sky,
Jupiter's emblem bird, with a lamb in its cruel talons,
and helpless shepherds pursue waving their arms, and their dogs
barking below watch as the bird flies out to sea.
Clearly, a splendid omen! Jason, cheered, sets out
to the palace of the proud and wicked king and encounters
Acastus, Pelias' son. That prince comes running to offer
the embraces of warm welcome a friend and cousin deserves.
190 "No, Acastus," the leader exclaims, "I do not come
to beg. You misconstrue my intentions. I know full well
that you are every bit as worthy as Telamon, Canthus,
Idas, or Castor to seek the fleece of Helle. Those long
roads we will travel beneath an endless expanse of sky
you will not have to endure. But when we return in triumph
and my vessel reunites me with Iolcos, the homeland I love,
what share will you have in our pride? Imagine your chagrin
as we are recounting tales of the trials and toils of our journey."

   Acastus, unable to bear any more, implores, "Enough!
200 I am ready to join. Let no man think me a coward or lazy!
Let me come with you to prove my prowess and share in the fame!
My too-solicitous father may disapprove, but my heart
is set and with you. And I shall contrive by stealth to join you
and take my place on shipboard when you put out to sea."
Thus he speaks, and the other, pleased for many reasons
to see such a display of courage, returns to the docks.

   There, meanwhile, the many Minyae are busy launching
the vessel, hauling away at the hawsers over their brawny
shoulders, and straining their backs and knees to heave and again
210 heave the ship, inch by inch, into the water,
where the sailors, panting and gasping, manage nevertheless
a celebratory cheer to the twang of Orpheus' lyre.
In joy they pile the altars high — chiefly to honor
you, Neptune, Lord of the Waters, but also the Winds,
whose grace they all invoke. To Glaucus, the shaggy sea god,
Ancaeus, Neptune's son, sacrifices an ox

decked with blue ribbons, and to Thetis he gives a heifer.
No one is more deft than he with the ritual axe
at the fat necks of cattle. Jason himself pours
a goblet in libation to the Lord of the Sea, saying,   220
"O god, who with a nod can stir the ocean to foam,
you, who with your salt water encompass the lands
of earth, hear my prayer and grant me your indulgence.
I am the first of mankind to venture forth on unlawful
paths across your waters, and therefore, one might suppose,
deserve the worst of your storms. It is not my own idea
to presume in this way, to pile mountain on high mountain
and summon down from Olympus bolts of heavenly lightning.
Pelias' prayers are false. Do not be swayed by his vows,
but know that he has devised and imposed his cruel commands   230
to send me off to Colchis and bring on me and my kin
the bitterest grief. I beg of you, therefore, mercy and justice.
Let your waters receive me: bear me up and protect
this ship and its crew of kings." Thus he spoke as he poured
the rich wine from the cup on the blazing coals of the fire.
    As the tongues of flame licking the sacrificial entrails
leapt up through the grate at the roasting gobbets of flesh of the bull,
Mopsus the holy prophet, standing there at the shoreline,
possessed of the god, shook his garlanded locks of hair
in the smart sea breeze and began to moan at the threshold of speech.   240
Men in their awe hushed one another and turned to hear him.
"Ah, what do I see? Neptune rouses himself,
having been summoned thus, or is he enraged by our daring?
He calls together the ocean's pantheon, that vast
assembly of the gods, and hears them crying aloud
as they clamor for him to defend the divine law. But Juno,
Juno herself comes to implore her mighty brother
for mercy. And she, Minerva, adds the weight of her words.
The gods of the sea have yielded! They grant their collective permission
to accept this vessel's encroachment. But I see a change in its fortune: 250
Hylas I see, but why does he cover his hair with rushes?
Why does he carry a pitcher? What is that blue he wears?
And Pollux, how did you get those wounds? Now I see bulls,
fierce, with flames from their nostrils. They plow furrows in earth

from which there are helmets sprouting, and spears of men at arms.
There is the fleece, but I see fighting, and . . . Who is this woman?
Why is she dreadfully covered in blood? She flies through the air
drawn by wingèd dragons and waving a bloodied sword!
Jason, save your children, snatch them away to safety . . .
260 I see a bridal chamber consumed in flames . . ." He stopped,
and the Minyae and their leader were stunned by his dismal vision,
but Idmon, Phoebus Apollo's son, was unperturbed
and stepped forward to share with the rest the gifts his father
had bestowed on him of haruspication and sortilege.
To Mopsus and the other comrades, he prophesied thus:
"As well as my father's lessons have enabled me to read
what the tongues of flame are saying, I see how the voyage will go:
with heavy toils and a heavier burden of griefs we must bear,
yet shall the ship overcome those obstacles it faces.
270 Be strong, I say, and brave, and struggle on to achieve
in the end the embrace of fathers and mothers welcoming home
their beloved sons." The tears that were running down his cheeks
his companions believed were of joy — but Idmon had seen that for him
there would be no such return: he was leaving Argos forever.

    Now Jason himself, their captain, spoke up: "You have heard his words
and know that we are allowed to hope for a happy ending
to the voyage we now commence if only you bring to our effort
that strength and courage each of your sires bred within you.
It is not my purpose here to question the tyrant's motives.
280 He has done us all the honor of setting us on this course,
but I cannot read his mind. Let us acknowledge this business
is that of the gods. The god who enjoins upon us a noble
adventure — Jupiter, Lord of the Gods, the world, and men —
has assigned us this awesome task: to institute commerce and shipping
throughout the civilized world. We who trust in his wisdom
may assuredly look to him for help in our tribulations,
which we shall recall in happy times as we tell our tales
to our grandsons. Meanwhile, we have this evening here. Enjoy
our last night at home of feasting and fellowship."
290 And they do enjoy themselves, on soft seaweed couches,
Hercules at their head, as the servants bring on the food,
sizzling meat on the skewers, and great panniers of bread.

Now from the crest of the mountain, Chiron comes, the centaur
holding up the stripling he has in his charge, Achilles,
who calls out to his father, Peleus, down on the beach.
The child sees his father startle at his familiar
voice, turn, grin, and stretch out his arms to embrace
his darling son and clutch him tight to his broad bosom.
The youngster takes no notice of the banquet table, the goblets
chased in precious metal, or the salvers piled with food,   300
but stares in delight at the armor, the captains' gleaming helmets,
and attends to their booming voices as if he were hearing music.
When Peleus sets him down, Achilles approaches the mighty
hero who sports the skin of a lion across his shoulder,
and he stares in delight and admiration at Hercules.
Peleus, altogether pleased, kisses the boy
and turns his face to the heavens to frame a prayer to the gods:
"I have heard the omens and offer thanks that you will grant
the following wind we want, but I ask that you keep him safe,
this remarkable boy of mine." And then he addresses Chiron: 310
"Give him whatever he needs. Teach him of warfare and let him
learn in the hunt the use of all his small-scale weapons.
Soon, when he has his strength, he will wield a spear like my own."
The men around him were cheered, and all were inspired with passion
and eager now for the voyage that they were about to dare,
the *Argo*'s passage over the deep blue water to fetch
the fleece of Phrixus' ram. They imagined it recovered
and brought to this very beach, and the prow and each of their foreheads
decked in celebratory clusters of sacred ivy.

The sun went down and daylight fled from the face of the water,   320
but the Minyae were making merry. Along the shore the lights
shone from the beach, a line of beacons, but out in the darkness
there was no eye yet to behold them. The bard from Thrace took up
his lyre and, easing the hours' passage, sang of Phrixus
and how he had stood before the sinful altar bound
with the ribbons of sacrifice, but then, at the last moment,
he and his sister Helle, who was running away from her cruel
stepmother, Ino, were wrapped in a cloud the heavens had sent
and together rode on the back of the marvelous golden ram
into the sky and eastward, grasping the animal's horns.   330

Seven times the dawn came up before them, and seven
times the moon rose and set. Sestos and Abydos, far
below them, looked like a single town on the Thracian shore,
but, tired, or giddy at that great height, Helle loosened
her grip and fell to the waves, where the weight of her waterlogged garments
dragged her under, and Phrixus looked back in horror to watch
her helpless thrashing and hear her choked cries for help
that finally faded to silence as her hair fanned out on the water.
 The last goblets were emptied. The men lay down to sleep —
340 all but Jason and agèd Aeson and Alcimede,
his father and mother, who gazed with brimming eyes at their son.
He tried as well as he could to soothe their troubled hearts,
and at length those two, exhausted, gave themselves over to sleep,
leaving Jason alone. To him the oaken mast
hewn from Chaonian Jupiter's sacred grove at Dodona
seemed to speak: "With you I venture forth to the ocean.
Not even the great goddess Minerva could have felled me
had I not been given the promise of a place at last in heaven.
Our time has come! We must bestir ourselves. We shall wander
350 over distant seas and beneath dark clouds of menacing skies,
but never give in to fear; trust in me and in heaven."
Thus it spoke, startling Jason, although he knew
the omen could not have been better. He sprang up from his bed
in agitation and looked to the east, where Tithonus' wife
was already touching the water with the delicate tints of dawn.
The Minyae now are awake, scurrying this way and that
on the deck as they prepare the rigging and check the rowlocks
from which the mighty oars will sweep the glassy water.
At last, from the lofty prow, Argus tautens the cable.
360 On shore, mothers are wailing and silent fathers are sick
at heart. They cling to one another in woeful embrace,
Alcimede's voice the loudest of all. Her keening laments
are to the other women's complaints like a blaring trumpet
all but drowning out a chorus of pipes of Pan.
The woman raves: "My son, you are going away to endure
hardships you have not at all deserved. I fear
for your life, but my spirit is not subdued. I pray to the gods
to keep you safe and implore the Fates to return you home.

If the cruel sea can be appeased by the prayers of troubled
mothers, I can endure the lonely days and the fears 370
of the long nights ahead. But if Fortune has other plans,
then I beg Death to show us his stern pity and take us,
burdened only with apprehensions but not with the anguish
of knowing that the worst has come to pass. Oh, woe!
I shall walk the beach and peer out at the tranquil sea and the sky
but take no joy in them, imagining Scythian shores
with their storm-lashed breakers attacking the shingle beneath a leaden
sky in which malevolent winds are forever wailing.
Give me a last embrace and speak those words I shall keep
in my ears. Close my weeping eyes with your dear fingers." 380
Thus did his mother mourn; his father, meanwhile, was brave
and tried to ease his son's discomfort at parting, saying:
"If only I had the strength of the old days when I fought
Pholus, the centaur who tried to fling the huge bowl at my head,
but there were a fair number of golden bowls at that feast
and I grabbed one even larger and hurled it and knocked him out.
If I were that man still, I'd be holding onto the bronze
stern of your ship, ready to climb aboard and row.
But if I cannot go myself, at least my prayers will be with you,
some of which are already answered. A ship of kings 390
sets forth, and my son is their captain, a leader of noble leaders.
I had my share of glory, but you will return one day,
the conqueror of Scythia's king and the Scythian ocean,
bearing upon your shoulders the fabulous golden fleece,
and I shall receive you with pride, as my fame gives way to yours."
So he spoke, and Jason embraced his distraught mother
collapsed upon his bosom while he felt his father's arm
along his broad shoulder and the sinewy hand on his neck.

And that was the end. The trumpet's last sad blast
had sounded to conclude the embrace and begin the voyage. 400
Each man of the crew takes his assigned place
and seizes his oar. To port, on the first bench Telamon sits,
and across from him, to starboard, taller, is Hercules.
The rest are arranged behind them: Asterion, whose father,
Cometes, had bathed him, newborn, in the rivers
where the turgid Enipeus flows into the Apidanus . . .

. . . .

... and on one bench Talaus flexes his rippling muscles,
while Leodocus from behind appears to be his shadow.
(Noble Argos had sent both of these men to Jason.)

410 Behind them is Idmon, ignoring the dire omens' message
and rejecting the shame that attaches to fear of the future. Next
is Iphitus, son of Naubolus, ready to cut through the water
with the shining blade of his oar. Euphemus, Neptune's son,
who lives in sea-washed Psamathe, is ready to ride his father's
heaving ocean. Deucalion, from Pella's sandy shore,
is next on the benches. (He is the accurate javelin thrower;
his identical twin brother, Amphion, a deadly man
in hand-to-hand combat, is also one of the rowers.)
Clymenus and his brother Iphiclus contribute

420 their great strength. And next is Nauplius — you know
his dismal story: his son, Palamedes, will one day
be unjustly accused at Troy and killed, and in rage
and grief the father will light along the coast deceptive
beacons to lure the Greeks returning home from the war,
so that he can watch them founder and drown. Caphareus is there,
and Oileus, to whom great sorrow will come — when Troy
has fallen, and his son Ajax will attempt to rape Cassandra,
for which offense the gods will punish him with Jove's
lightning bolt. Cepheus, too, is there, a comrade

430 of Hercules when he killed the huge boar on the slopes
of Erymanthus. Who else? The muster roll goes on,
a rich cluster of proper nouns to roll in the mouth.
Amphidamas was one of the mariners, and long-haired
Eurytion, and Nestor who signed on to this first
voyage for glory and years later, amazed, would behold
an entire ocean covered in white by Argive sails
heading for Troy. And here is Mopsus, the great seer,
Phoebus' son and Manto's, wearing the flowing white
robe that reaches down to his boots and the curious helmet

440 adorned with ribbons and laurel leaves his father loves
from the banks of Thessaly's Peneus River. On Hercules' side
is Tydeus, strong at the oar, and Periclymenus, son
of Neleus, the boxer who broke his opponents' faces

at Elis, rich in horses, and Methone and Aulon.
And you, Philoctetes, son of Poeas, are rowing to Colchis.
Famous now for your use of your father's mighty spear,
you will be better known one day for Hercules' arrows.
On the same side is Butes, whose hives on the Attic shore
send out to Hymettus' flowery slopes their busy swarms
with an eerie monotone buzz. And next is Phalerus—his   450
arm is tattooed with the serpent that slipped from the spreading tree
and was coiled around him, ready to strike when he was a child,
but Alcon, his father, holds his uncertain bow and the arrow
he hopes will kill the snake but leave the boy alive
and in fact not even scratched. And Eribotes is here,
and Peleus, who trusts in the goodwill of his in-laws
and of his wife—they are all gods and goddesses. High
on the prow is the gleaming head of the spear of Peleus. He
is Aeacus' son, and the shaft of his weapon is taller than others
as the ash from which it was fashioned was taller than other trees   460
in the grove on Pelion's slope. Menoetius, Actor's son,
is here, having left his son Patroclus in Chiron's cave
with young Achilles, his playmate. There they learn to ride
on the back of Chiron, the genial centaur who teaches the boys
to hurl the light spear and to pluck the strings of the lyre.
Phlias is one of the crew, a son of the shaggy god,
which may be why he wears his own hair long and flowing.
Ancaeus is here as well, whose father was the sea god,
and his mother, Astypalaea, now that he is aboard
puts her trust in the tenderness of Neptune. His half-brother   470
Erginus is also sanguine, supposing that their father
will take good care and protect him. He also knows the guile
of water at night and of winds that come up sometimes out of nowhere
or out of Aeolus' cave. He is the man whom Tiphys,
the *Argo*'s pilot, trusts when his eyes are bleary from gazing
at the Lesser Bear in the sky, to take a watch at the helm.
Oebalus' grandson Pollux, the hero of Sparta, is also
one of their number: he wears on his fists the bull-hide cestus
with metal studs that can kill—as if he would box the winds
that carry along the Pagasean vessel. His brother Castor   480
is here, who prefers the breaking and riding of horses. His favorite

stallion, Cyllarus, is left to graze in Amyclae's meadows
until he returns from this quest for the fleece of the beast from which
Helle took that fatal fall. Both brothers are wearing
rich cloaks dyed with Taenarian purple their mother,
Leda, wove on her looms. On each is a scene of Taygetus'
slopes with their bosky woods, and, traced in gold at the bottom,
a cunning representation of Eurotas' turbulent stream.
Then on each is the hero riding a snow-white horse,
490   and one can see on the chests their father's swan-feather emblem.
And you, Meleager, your rich tunic keeps coming unclasped
to reveal your broad shoulders and splendid pectoral muscles
matched only by those of Hercules himself.

    Tired? Beginning to flag? Valerius has his second
wind and is off on a tear now. He lists Mercury's sons:
Aethalides first, the archer; Eurytus, good with the sword
he can use like a machete clearing a path through brush;
Echion, the boatswain, respected among the Minyae;
and Iphis . . . your ashes the *Argo* will leave behind on the sad
500   Scythian shore (and those on your bench will miss you and mourn).
Admetus is here, from Pherae, you whom for a time
Apollo served as a shepherd and offered eternal life
if you could find another to pay your debt to Hades.
(The god of Delos would tend your flocks, and his sister, Diana,
wept to see him look for a place in the shade on Ossa's
foothills or slake his thirst with the waters of Lake Boebeius.)
Who's left? Canthus, Abas' son, who leans over the thwarts
to churn the waves with his oar. He will never come home again,
for one day a spear will bring him down in the dust on the isle
510   of Aeaea, but now he is all strength and hope and glory
as bright as the fancy shield he bears that his father gave him
showing Euripus' waters and Neptune rising up
from oyster-rich Geraestus, riding a chariot drawn
by a brace of his savage sea wolves. And neither will Polyphemus
return to give the signal for which his servants have waited —
to set the torch to his father's funeral pyre. (No,
this isn't the famous Cyclops; this is the other, the son
of Eilatus, king of somewhere or other. The names that once
had meaning are wearing away to the bare phonemes. Time's

passage is stupefying, and epics, if they delay, 520
cannot prevent forever the ruin they ought to defy.)
We're nearly done. Here's Idas, hauling away at his oar
that bites the blue-green water. He sits on the last bench.
His brother, the keen-eyed Lynceus, is excused from having to row,
for he can see through solid objects, look down through the earth
and make out the Styx's secrets, or, helping the helmsman, read
the stars on nights when Jupiter's clouds obscure the sky,
and keep the ship on course. Zetes and Calais, sons
of Boreas, from Thrace, don't have to work as oarsmen
either—they are the ones who trim the sails and adjust 530
the rigging that sings in the spars. Orpheus, also from Thrace,
is never required to row but provides the rhythmic music
that sets the stroke and keeps the oars from fouling each other.
Agèd Iphiclus too has drawn a pass: his job
is to give advice and help maintain the crew's morale
when difficulty or danger demands that men remember
who they are and what their lineage now requires.
Finally (can you believe it?) Argus, who built the ship,
is in charge of repairs: he sees that the strakes are well-enough caulked,
maintains the vessel, and keeps it seaworthy and sound. 540
    Tiphys has checked the charts and set the course, and Jason
sees at the last minute Pelias' son, Acastus.
His javelins in hand and sporting a glittering shield,
he comes running down the beach, splashes into the water,
and climbs aboard. Jason raises his sharp sword high
and it catches the sun as it falls to cut the hawser. The ship,
like a huntsman deep in the forest who has raided a tiger's lair
and snatched the cubs he clasps to his breast as he flees the fierce
mother whose rage he'd rather not have to face, is off
and running to measured strokes of the banks of sweeping oars. 550
On shore, the mothers stand and stare, as sorrow and pride
slosh in their hearts together, and they watch the vessel move.
They can see the sails and make out the glittering shields of the heroes
that gleam in the sunlight, beacons flashing. But farther and farther
the *Argo* seems smaller as space overwhelms it and even the mast
dwindles down to a mote in the eye and at last disappears.
    Then, from his citadel in the stars, the Father of Gods,

glad at heart, looked down to behold these heroes of Greece
and approve their glorious efforts. In his father's time, when Saturn
560　ruled the cosmos, effort had not been demanded of men.
But here the Fates had marked the dawn of a great new age
of achievement from which might come prosperous civilization,
and the gods in their thrones rejoiced. But Sol was not content
and from his troubled bosom poured forth these words of complaint:
"O Zeus, supreme creator and Lord of Olympus, hear me!
You who regulate planets and the course of the changing seasons,
can this be part of your plan? Do you approve such a venture
with all the Greeks sailing across the sea? I rise
to object and offer my just complaint. We had struck a bargain!
570　That no one might have cause to envy my son Aeëtes,
I chose for him no prosperous island like Teucer's Cyprus,
no fertile Peloponnese, but a distant, frigid region
where rivers are bound in ice at the end of the earth. From there
still would the son of the Sun have retreated, but dense miasmas
beyond were too opaque for light to penetrate. Savage,
cold, and remote, that region cannot have given offense
or in any way provoked the Greeks to adventure there.
What complaint have the Minyae who, neither invited nor welcome,
venture toward the Phasis' forbidding banks? The exile
580　Phrixus came there, true, but my son did not join with him
in an expedition for vengeance but invited him rather to wed
and dwell among our people, united by marriage and blood.
I ask that the ship be stopped. Turn it back. Do not
permit the Greeks to intrude on our sea to bring us further
harm! Each day, I look down at the coast of the Adriatic
where poplar trees that were once my daughters sough in the wind
at the mouth of the Po in mourning for Phaethon's ruin. My portion
is bitter enough . . ." He stopped, but the Lord of War arose
in support, for the fleece was hanging in one of his shrines as a trophy.
590　In opposition Juno spoke in Jason's behalf
as Minerva also argued, but then the Father of Gods
pronounced his judgment: "All this has been decreed from the start
of time, and events that now move forward run in their destined
courses. I have founded a line of kings to last
throughout the ages. Now I reveal to you the plan

I have drawn up disposing the various lands of the earth.
That great stretch of the East from the Hellespont on as far
as the River Don, rich in horses and famous for fierce
fighters, no men have ever dared until now to challenge.
That time draws to an end, as Asia's moment wanes 600
and the Greeks, coming into their strength and prosperity, venture forth
to claim my favor. My sacred oak trees, the vatic tripods,
and all the shades of their forebears have launched them onto the sea.
For Bellona, the Goddess of War, a path has been cleared through the water,
the storm at the end of the storms these brave mariners face.
More than sheepskin will Asia lose, for the Greeks will take
a princess, and then in turn from Ida's slopes there will come
a shepherd prince to capture a queen and bring lamenting,
rage, bloodshed, and death to many heroes. My mind
is fixed on this — the daring, the striving of many men 610
when the sea shall be full of ships of former suitors courting
glory. Mycenae shall shiver in bivouac at Troy,
and many sons of men and sons of gods will perish
as Asia yields at last to forces of Europe and fate.
For Danaans, too, I see that the end is not far off,
as I turn my favor again elsewhere to other nations
for whom the bounty of earth will offer itself from mountains,
forests, lakes, and plains, and the oceans will open themselves.
In the balance of hopes and fears shall every people be tried
as I determine who shall prosper and who shall fail, 620
and which should rule over which, as I bestow the reins
of power in men's affairs." Then the Father of Gods
turns his eyes to the blue Aegean and speaks to his sons,
to Hercules and Leda's children, Castor and Pollux.
"Reach for the stars, my lads, and acquit yourselves as heroes.
It was only after the struggle on Phlegra's field that I
could establish here on Olympus' top this palace of gods.
The path to heaven is painful, as Bacchus knows, and Apollo,
who have undergone those hardships that proved their divine mettle
and were made for a time to wander the rocky roads of the earth." 630
So he spoke, and he hurled a thunderbolt that blazed
through the clouds down to the earth where, over the *Argo*, it split
to strike both Castor and Pollux: miraculously harmless,

what it did was make them glow with an eerie radiance crewmen
would never forget and later invoke in times of crisis.

    Boreas, meanwhile, from Mount Pangaeus' fastness espies
the sails on the sea, and off in a huff he goes at once
to Sicily's coast and the rocky Lipari Islands of Aeolus'
savage kingdom. His progress flattens crops in his path,
640   and mighty forests groan at his wings' turbulent eddies.
Opposite Cape Faro's cliff, where the spray flies high
and then falls back to dismaying depths that terrify sailors,
are the islands, home to the squalls and storms that batter boats.
Acamas and Pyragmon live here; in days gone by,
they would make mischief and vent their fury across the wide
expanses of ocean. (Aeolus had not yet become their master.
This was the ancient time when Gibraltar had not yet broken
from Africa's shore to form that strait, and before Messina's
passageway had been carved by the violent waves of the sea.)
650   Jupiter, in thunder, appointed Aeolus king
to govern — as well as he could — their wildness. He confines them
in caves of rock with gates of iron but, when their roaring
reaches a certain pitch and he can no longer control them,
he unbars the doors and permits them to wander and howl until,
exhausted at last, they subside. To Aeolus' lofty throne
Boreas came to deliver his urgent news: "A ship!
I have seen with my own eyes what the Greeks have made with axes,
a wooden thing with cloth that catches my winds and employs them,
making me the servant of mere mortals. They know
660   it is not given to me to stir the sea from its bottom
to overwhelm their ship, and therefore are they emboldened.
But you can give me the power to destroy their presumptuous vessel.
My own sons are aboard, but for Zetes' and Calais' sakes
I am in no way moved. Grant that this threat of men
to our sovereignty may meet with appropriate retribution
before they have spread their menace by demonstrating to others,
beyond Thessaly's shores, these powers of human craft."

    The sound of his voice had scarcely faded away in the air
when the winds arose to clamor for release to the open sea.
670   Aeolus opened the gate wide and they burst out, West Wind
and South Wind together, their black wings beating the air, and East Wind,

his hair a wild tangle and his nose and mouth covered up
for protection against sandstorms. They inaugurated the tempest
that drove the whitecapped waves onshore while it filled the sky
with clouds as black as night that lightning suddenly sundered.
At sea, the *Argo's* prow shudders and shakes, and the oars
are torn from the rowers' hands by waves that pummel the hull
in rage. A gusting wind rips the sails from the waving
mast, and the tatters and shreds that remain on the spars flutter,
flags of surrender. The hearts of the Minyae are filled with dread   680
and the brave sailors tremble as lightning flashes and fades
to show the ship in its crazy pitching and yawing. The yardarm
catches crabs in the turbulent water. This isn't nature,
the way of the sea, as the sailors try hard to believe,
but the doing of angry gods. In either case, their fear
prompts them to wail in dismay: "Is this why our forebears shunned
the ocean? Is this what happens when men profane the deeps?
We have scarcely cleared the harbor, and we have to face this fury
of wind and water and darkness and hidden reefs and rocks!
Each moment is worse than the one we have just survived. Beware   690
impiety, pride, and madness! And beware the terrible sea!"
     What can they do? Even Hercules falls silent. He stares at his mighty
club and his quiver of arrows, useless now. The others
are mumbling desperate prayers or clinging to one another
as they watch in horror the timbers give way and the ship spring leaks.
It is taking water, thirsty gulps of the brine, as the angry
East Wind lashes and South Wind roars in antiphonal anger.
And then, as if in answer, West Wind takes up the cry,
and the waters boil while Neptune, armed with his trident spear,
raises his shaggy head from the dark blue depths to command: 700
"Let the ship pass! My sister Juno has asked it, and Pallas,
and my heart gives way to their piteous tears. Vessels will come
and go this way and that, from Pharos and Tyre, and suppose
the strange thing they do is permitted and take for granted
their bold assertions of will. Sails will unfurl on the sea lanes
that South Wind will shred to tatters, and men will cry out in terror
to beg for their lives, the most devout of all human prayers.
In error will men blame my son Orion for storms,
and the Pleiades that shine in Taurus' train, but the fault

710 is there in the arrogant *Argo* where Tiphys stands at the helm
and plots a course of grief for sailors' widows and orphans
who will curse your names and pray that you rot in hell forever."
Saying this, he ordered South Wind to abate and return
to Aeolus' keeping; he lulled the heaving billows of ocean
that crashed on the rocky shores, and the rain, at his bidding, moved
away as the clouds dispersed. In the gentled sky, a rainbow
shone over the vessel that rode the sparkling sea
as Thetis and her father Nereus bore it along
supporting it with his mighty arms beneath its hull,

720 in thanks for which the *Argo*'s captain put on his prayer shawl
and took up Aeson's goblet—this was Salmoneus' gift
before that king went mad and set himself up as a rival
to Jove, trying to fashion lightning bolts to fling
from mountaintops (he managed to ruin Pisa's forests
and burned the fields of Elis). Jason took up that cup
and poured a libation of wine into the sea, praying:
"O you gods, who rule the waters and have domain
over the winds and their storms; you whose dwelling places
reach from the ocean's depths to the heights of heaven; and you,

730 Father of Gods who order the spheres of the sky and govern
the tides, behold a novelty here on earth, a ship
on the sea with armed men. For your rage I make atonement
and pray you look with indulgence upon us. Let me bring
these men safely to shore, and let me go home again
where I shall offer up on the sacrificial altars
those rich feasts your mercy shall have deserved. In every
village and hamlet men shall acknowledge the might of Neptune
and pay you honor." Thus were his words, and his shipmates offered
a shout of boisterous approval, their hands raised over their heads

740 in supplication. On shore, meanwhile, the farmers, unable
to guess any other cause for this out-of-season tempest,
have gathered together to pray and offer vows their priests
have recommended. But then the weather turns, and they see
the sky clear and the day grow gentle. At sea, the ship
is flying along, its prow cutting through waves, its stern
leaving a widening wake. Tiphys has taken the helm

and men have been quick to make sail, looking to him as, above,
thunder, winds, and rainstorms are alert to the wishes of Jove.

Now, in the first moment he has for reflection, Jason
finds himself uneasy. Having accepted Acastus,   750
he may have made a mistake and invited Pelias' anger.
What will that tyrant do? What punishment may he impose
on Jason's parents, left behind and defenseless now
that their son is gone? He tries to reason his fears away,
but Pelias' spiteful nature is a blunt and brutal fact.

Meanwhile, back in Iolchos, Pelias, full of rage,
has climbed a mountain peak from which to watch the ship
disappear in the offing. What can he do in his fury?
How can he cause them hurt? What good is courage or power
when the huge margin of blue of the sea protects those villains?   760
He thinks how Daedalus soared into the air from Ida's
top in Crete with Icarus close behind him, while Minos'
soldiers cried out in fury to see his escape in the sky
and into the clouds, and the horsemen took off and tried to follow,
peering up, but the heavens were empty, and they returned
to barracks at Gortyn, their quivers still full and their hearts
heavy with anger and shame. He returns to the palace to wander
in Prince Acastus' rooms, and stretches out on the floor
to kiss with his lips the places where his son's feet would walk . . .
But not any more! He shakes his white-haired head in grief   770
and incomprehension, and sighs and groans, and complains aloud:
"Are you, too, filled with sorrow, grieving for me as I grieve
for you, my son? I see you, surrounded by treacherous men,
ready, each one, to betray you as you meet the thousand dangers
of the ruinous venture as far as the Pontus and Scythia's wastes!
I sent them on this goose chase, and they, in turn, trapped you
with an empty offer of glory you'll never enjoy. But for me
the grief is all too real. You'll never get past those straits!
Had I thought it might be done, I'd have given the chance to you,
and the men and the ships. But certain destruction is what they face,   780
and you, too, now, my own dear boy . . ." He spoke in a frenzy,
"Jason! You aren't as safe as you think, for I can cause you
grievous pain. You have my son? I have your father!

And rivers of bitter tears like mine shall wet your cheeks."
He wanders around the palace, muttering, scheming, and plotting
whatever mischief he can devise. Lycurgus, king
of Thrace, was like that once, with murder in his heart
when Bacchus had driven his thirsty subjects into rebellion,
and his wife and child ran for their lives, fleeing before him
790   as he pursued them, distraught, down the long colonnades of his palace.
      At that same moment, Jason's mother Alcimede
was offering up to the Lord of the Underworld and his shades
the ritual gifts in the hope that the summoned ghosts might tell her
news of her son. And Aeson, less given to superstition,
but just as eager to know, has joined with his wife to perform
the bloody rite: the trench is brimming with blood and herbs,
and the old woman invokes her ancestors and the god
Mercury, who acts as the medium to the dead.
She moans, mutters, and hums, and in answer Aeson's father,
800   Cretheus, appears, an insubstantial face,
but it's recognizably he. He gazes at his son
and daughter-in-law and, after he sips the enabling blood
they have poured into the ditch, speaks: "Do not be afraid!
Jason is well. He flies over the blue water
drawing ever closer to Colchis. Aea's townsmen
read the omens of heaven and hear their soothsayers' words
in dismay but cannot be certain what to believe. Your son
will arrive, the terror of nations, and return with glorious spoils
and a Scythian bride as well. Then would I come back to life
810   to forestall what will happen . . ." He hesitates here for a moment
but then resumes: "Meanwhile, a violent king is plotting
against your lives. Your brother is given over to passion
and murder is in his heart. Flee for your lives! Or flee
from your enfeebled limbs by killing yourselves. Escape!
I tell you that throngs of the dead call out to you to join them
in the sacred glades where the winds of Aeolus, my father,
sweep in random gusts their incorporeal wraiths."
      In the palace halls, the servants cried out in fear and despair,
and the city buzzed with rumors: *The king is mustering troops,*
820   *thousands of them; the priests abandon their smoking altars*
and put aside their robes. What will become of us? Aeson

could not think what to do. A lion, surrounded by beaters,
yawns in his hesitation and blinks his yellowy eyes.
So it was with Aeson. Should he bother to take up a sword
and pretend to youth and strength? Should he try to raise an army
of friends? (They are all old men.) Or go to the streets to the rabble?
Putting her arms around him, his wife implores: "Be steady.
Whatever may come, I am here by your side, sharing your fate.
I will not deign to prolong my life or look upon Jason's
face unless with you. When our son departed, I said   830
I was ready then to die. We can bear whatever may come."
Death itself is not the question but how it happens,
and Aeson considers what right and proper end of his life
he can contrive, a conclusion suitably noble and worthy
of Aeolus' line. He also thinks of his younger son,
a stripling for whom he would be a model of courage and honor
the boy might remember in love and pride as long as he lived.
Aeson then led his wife and son to the sacred grove
of ancient cypress trees near the altar, a solemn place
where the daylight filtered down through the leaves to a constant gloom.   840
Grazing there was a bull, a consecrated beast
with the blue ribbons wound about his horns and yew
wreathed on his brow. Skittish, panting, pawing the ground
as if he understood he was facing death, the bull
had been reprieved for the moment as the frightened priests had fled.
One might have supposed that the beast had been saved for Aeson's use.
With one hand on the horn of the victim, Aeson spoke
for the last time, addressing his ancestors and gods:
"You who received from mighty Jove the gift of light
and whose names still resound on earth for your fortunate reigns,   850
your wisdom in council and valor in war, your heirs remember
each of you with reverence. And you, my beloved father,
summoned as you have been to witness my death and endure
yet again the all but forgotten sorrows of flesh,
welcome me now to your dim and quiet world. Accept
this offering I send before me. You, Astraea,
Goddess of Justice, and you, the Eumenides, who avenge
transgressions of gods' laws, and Themis, whose retribution
all men ought to fear, attend on Pelias' wicked

860 house. Visit upon him your cleansing torches and fill him
with fear: let him understand that Jason will not come home
alone, but hordes of Asians, crazed, will be following hard
and looking for vengeance. Let him walk the shore and worry
that the force of these hostile princes may overwhelm his own.
Let him behold in terror the heroes returning in triumph
and let his schemes for protection be endless and all in vain.
Jason shall parade the golden fleece, and my spirit
will gloat as Pelias cringes. But let his end be shameful,
not by the hand of a soldier in the light of day, but secret,
870 wretched, as women, his kinfolk, do him to shameful death.
Let it be painful and also absurd, as those he has trusted
turn on him, betraying, tearing him limb from limb
in a madness that does not leave fragments enough for a tomb.
This is my dying prayer, that he be made to pay
for having sent my son and his brave companions to sea."
Then he addresses Hecate and intones the prescribed prayer
to Charon, the spell that backward and forward signals the endless
crossings he makes to carry the spirits this way and that.
Standing beside him now, he senses the three Furies,
880 the chief of whom takes the cup with the deadly blood from his hand
and drinks, then Alcimede takes her turn, and at last
Aeson takes it back from her trembling hands and drains it.
    A sudden noise! There are Pelias' soldiers rushing in,
their weapons drawn, but useless for Aeson's corpse and his wife's.
There is only the little boy, terrified by his parents'
death he has just beheld. The soldiers show him no mercy
but hack him at once to pieces, reuniting him thus
with his mother and father, whose ghosts shudder a moment in grief
but then ascend to the gentle clouds in a silent sky.
890   Far below, removed from the world of light, is the deep
realm of Tartarus. There dwells wide-mouthed Chaos, whose maw
could swallow all of matter. It is said there are two doors
through which our shades may enter, one of which stands open
all the time, and men may enter, entire nations
and even the greatest kings. The other, no one attempts
or even tries to unbar, but now and again it opens
spontaneously, flies wide to receive a hero whose wounds

on his breast are decorations. A man of honor whose life
he gave to his fellow man or, sometimes, a robed priest
may attain this rare distinction. Mercury ushers them in,   900
lighting their way with a torch he wields as they tread the path
to the fields of bliss in an endless sunlight of celebration,
a continual singing and dancing in amity and in peace.
Into this happy beyond, Aeson leads his wife
and young son. He shows them what torments Pelias faces,
pointing out the other gate where monstrous creatures
lurk at the threshold. Awesome, those dreadful specters, and awesome
but utterly different, these precincts of blessings, ease, and joy.

Book II

Meanwhile, Jason, entirely unaware of these crimes
and as yet untouched by their grief, slices his way through the sea,
for Juno has not allowed that the hero even suspect,
lest he should turn about and, leaving undone those deeds
heaven has destined for him, hurl himself in rage
at Pelias, that guilty uncle who sprawls on the usurped throne.
    They are making headway, passing Pelion with its verdant
crown of mountain ash and drawing abeam of Diana's
temple at Tisaeum, which disappears in their wake
along with Skiathos Island. They round Sepias' cape
and glide by Thessaly's plains where horses enjoy good grazing.
They have the town and river of Amyros now abaft
and can just make out the Dolopian grave mounds. Reefing the sails
from the offshore winds from the river's mouth, they heave at the oars
to the next checkpoint, which is Eurymenae, and South Wind there
returns to belly the sails and churn the water to whitecaps
as the Minyae make way seaward and Ossa fades behind them
to disappear in the clouds. They reach the bay at Pallene
where the gods and giants fought, and the huge rocks that remain,
the missiles they hurled at each other, suggest what that combat was like.
On all sides were the mountains, the giants their mother earth
had, in her pity, clothed where they lay with verdant trees,
and their crags still seemed to reach upward, as even yet
their crouching figures threaten or cower before the gods.
Their father, meanwhile, buffets their flanks with his storms and flings
bolt after deadly bolt at their hulking shapes from the angry

skies. Their chief, however, is not to be found among them,
Typhoeus—buried alive beneath the Sicilian dirt.
The story that men tell is that Neptune grabbed his hair
and dragged him out to sea where he thrashed in the water, flailing   30
and churning the waves with his snaky limbs, and the sea god piled
great Aetna on his head with the cities along her flank,
and still he heaves in his pain and rage as he shakes that mountain
and all of Sicily shudders as he beats at its very foundation,
shifting its crushing burden that falls back onto his chest,
and he—or it—produces a groan of baffled despair.
　　Now Hyperion's car was approaching the Irish Sea
where the god lets the reins go slack as the day's journey is ending.
This was the hour when Tethys extends her arms to embrace
the Lord of the Ocean, the mighty Titan who in his rage   40
shivers the bed of the sea, producing a sloshing of waves
and spume onshore. The sailors' fears gripped them as darkness
covered the face of heaven and hid the coastal mountains,
and then, from the silent constellations, meteors fell
in vague but baleful omen. As a traveler might, on a road
at night in an unfamiliar place, look this way and that
with his ears straining and eyes peering into the darkness
of the trees on either side with their thick, menacing shadows
where every woeful fancy seems to assail him, so
did the heroes feel afraid, but Hagnius' son, Tiphys,   50
the ship's pilot, spoke in comfort with words of courage:
"We do not go alone without the help of the gods,
nor do I steer our course by my own wits: Minerva,
the Tritonian queen who first taught me my craft, even now
offers me aid and directs our keel. We have come this far
and survived our first great storm! How many times did the mounting
waves batter our frail vessel? But through her skill,
even that tenth wave all sailors dread fell harmless.
Courage, my friends! You see the clear sky overhead,
and Cynthia's moon with its delicate horns has appeared—no tinge   60
of menacing red to imply foul weather. The sun went down
cleanly into the water, and that, too, was auspicious.
The wind has picked up to belly our sail and speed our vessel
through the dark and silent hours. By Minerva's teaching I choose

those stars that do not rise and set by which to take
my bearings. Mark how Orion sinks into the sea.
You can almost hear the hissing as Perseus touches the water.
I look, instead, to the steady pole star by which I plot
our course, in the writhing Serpent that enfolds its seven stars."
70   Thus he spoke and showed them the various constellations,
the Hyades, and Orion, and the brightly shining Boötes.
From this they all took heart, and then, to renew their bodies,
they took some bread, the gift of Ceres, and washed it down
with a swallow or two of wine. Sleep then overcame them,
and the ship sailed on with a following wind under kindly stars.

    Now in the east, Aurora stirs and her first faint light
softens the sky and, on land, the thickness of night's black
relents. From the cowering sheepfolds, the prowling bears retreat
to their dank dens as the shorebirds venture forth to scan
80   the lines of the surf. Then gleams from Phoebus' fiery horses
break over Athos' peak and fling out the day like a mat
that covers land and water. The rowers pull at their oars
and the prow cuts through the water with a steady snore. Now Lemnos,
Vulcan's island abode, raises its head from the waves.
O Lord of Fire, how great were the sufferings you there endured
from women in their ambition or faithlessness — and yet
to Lemnos still you return for the sake of its people's kindness.

    Long ago when Jupiter first learned of the plot
of the other gods, jealous of him in his newly won
90   authority, he showed his righteous anger to Juno,
his sister and wife, and hung her high in the sky. In terror
she stared down to the deep abyss into which she would plummet,
but Vulcan appeared to save his mother and would have unbound her
had Jupiter not interfered and cast him down from the heavens
to fall all day and the next, and for nine days to keep falling
to crash at last on Lemnos' shore, where his groans of pain
alerted the men of the city, who found him sprawled on the rocks,
showed him their pity, and nursed him until, on crippled knees,
he was able to take his first painful and tentative steps.
100   Here, ever since his father allowed his return to heaven's
glories, Vulcan has come — to Lemnos, as dear to his heart
as Aetna or his Liparean summer places, for here

he has established his temples in which he likes to appear
when he has completed work on a shield or a thunderbolt
he has made for his mighty father. But the altar there to Venus
is cold and has never been used since the day that goddess trembled
at her husband's justifiable wrath, when Vulcan bound her
and Mars together in snares he had set to trap the lovers.
And since that moment Venus has hated the people of Lemnos,
plotting against them in wicked schemes to contrive their ruin.   110
She who can be so gentle, who plaits her silken hair
with a golden pin and whose robes flow so rich and easy,
can change in an instant, her cheeks going blotchy and dark with rage,
and she is a Fury clad in black and bent on vengeance,
the smoke of her torch acrid enough to make one weep.
Thus it was when the men of Lemnos routed the Thracians
and made their wickerwork boats covered in animal hides
to bring back to their island the plunder of battle, the livestock
and the women of Thrace to be slaves in their households at home.
Amused they were by their prisoners' strange clothes and outlandish   120
necklaces, and happy, bantering over the water
from one boat to the next how their wives would all be pleased
to welcome their husbands home and be freed from their boring chores
by these women, the prizes of war. But, out of the blue,
Venus came down to earth wrapped in a dismal cloud
to make way for Rumor, whom Jove had banished from heaven
but whose voice yet resounds on earth, spreading good news
and bad to stir the hearts of men or seize them with panic.
Resentful and angry, she lives neither in heaven nor hell,
but bothers the earth. Wise men know to mistrust her reports,   130
but even they give way, for she can assail a city
and the wagging of busy tongues will shake the stones of its buildings.
This was exactly what Venus wanted, and Rumor, summoned,
appeared at once, ready and eager to do her bidding.
The goddess eggs her on: "Make all haste to Lemnos
to work your mischief there in the heart of every household.
Just as you do when you whisper that war is about to break out,
spreading your stories of trumpets and snorting steeds and soldiers
countless upon the plain, speak to their secret fears
and tell them how their husbands are coming home with women,   140

lascivious concubines who have made their captors captives
of foreign erotic refinements too shameful for decent women
even to try to imagine. Let their resentments fester
and madden every one of the Lemnian wives. Then I
will come, myself, to exploit what you have so well prepared."

    The other departs forthwith and goes to the heart of the city.
There she greets Eurynome, Codrus' wife, who has waited
faithful all this time to her husband and marriage vows.
She and her women servants have kept themselves busy spinning
150   and weaving, piling up bolts of fabric and counting the days
and endless nights. To her, in the guise of Neaera, the goddess
comes in sobs and tears with her cheeks clawed as in grief
to complain: "If only the news I deliver were not so grim!
If only the tears I shed could wash away our sorrows!
The truth is that your husband, to whom you have always been true
and for whose return you have prayed, is coming home to shame you,
a slave to his lust for some Thracian woman, a battle trophy.
No match for you in looks or in skills of spinning and weaving,
'nothing like you in honor or chastity, ill bred,
160   she cannot boast, as you do, of such distinguished forebears
as Doryclus. Her only distinction is on her cheek
where the hot brand made its mark. What can you possibly do?
Where can you go with your children? Or how can you stay on here,
having to share your man with another wife, a rival?
A life like that is a torment with you and your children, wretched
and even in danger of poison with every bite and sip.
They are proud people, the Dahae, but unlike us, untrammeled
by civilization's restraints. Reared on the steppes of Asia
and fed with the milk of untamed beasts, they are all bloodthirsty,
170   capricious, headstrong people, and they will be living among us.
Rumor has it that my own husband has one of these women,
some tattooed semisavage snatched from a nomad's wagon
and dragged here to supplant me in my household and bed."
That was enough. She stopped, for the other was now in tears
and quaking in fear. She moved on to speak in Iphinoë's ear,
and kindle similar flames in Amythaon's heart
and Olenius'. And on through the town she proceeds, crying
to one and all that their faithless husbands are plotting to drive them

out of their homes, and that Thracian women will take their places.
Jealousy mixes with anger and fear as the women confer,   180
and none of them disbelieves or thinks to question the story,
which every retelling confirms. They call upon various gods
and goddesses in their shrill lament and they take to their beds
or wander about their houses as if to bid good-bye
to the lives they are sure they are losing. Hysterical, angry, bereft,
they rush from their husbands' dwellings to throng together for comfort,
bewailing their common complaint beneath the impassive stars,
each of them ruing the day she was married and cursing her husband
upon whose head she calls down the hottest fires of hell.

    First among the complainers is Venus, the goddess, disguised   190
as Dryope, whose bitter reproaches and keenings are endless:
"I had rather be one of the conquered, a Sarmatian woman
enduring defeat and shame and gazing into the flames
destroying my father's house or watching the conquerors loot
the temples we built for our gods. Are they worse off than we?
Does that beast to whom I am married think now to subject me
to mortification? Am I to become my servant's servant?
Or do I flee the city and leave my own children behind?
I say we must arm ourselves with swords and burning torches
and, as they lie down in their beds in which we have been supplanted,   200
let us do some drastic and splendid deed our affronted
love may prompt! Let Venus inspire us in our action!"
She glared into their faces as if to ignite with her eyes
a fire in each of their souls. The babes at her bosom, worn
as props for this very gesture, she flung down to the ground
in an act of madness by which she inspired in all the others
a similar recklessness. Roused, maddened, their hearts
now hard and filled with pride from her words, they are swept away
as they gaze out at the empty sea. They make a convincing
show of welcome, rehearsing their dance and decking the temples   210
with gay festoons of woven flowers. With loving smiles
they greet their returning husbands and lead them back to their dwellings
for the homecoming celebration, the feasting and drinking of wine.
Think of Tisiphone's terrible torture of Theseus, tasting
the dainties that he and Phlegyas had on the table before them,
that food she had touched defiled, a mass of wriggling serpents.

Venus whirls a pine torch over her head and smoke
swirls about her, gloom in the gloom in dismal portent,
as she descends to Lemnos, ushered by peals of lightning
220   from towering banks of clouds. With her father's pomp and glory
she flies through the air and utters a shrill cry of distracted
rage to make the heights of Athos away on the mainland
shudder and then in the echo slosh the sea in its bed.
Children in their cradles quaked in terror and mothers
felt a sudden chill. Fear and Getic Discord,
together with Treachery, Fury, and, leading them all, Death,
convened at that strident summons, ready to do their worst.
But Venus with her own hands engineered the dreadful crime.
She it was who produced that continuo of groans
230   and the harmonizing tune of cries of men struck down.
Rushing into houses with the head of a man still streaming
blood that stained her gown, her hair as wild as her victim's,
she proclaimed, "I have avenged that guilt that stained my bed."
With her troupe of ghastly attendants, she forced her way into bedrooms,
placed swords in the fearful or even reluctant hands,
and urged the women on. (How can I write this down,
these appalling scenes of violence and the deaths of all these men?
What is a gentle poet to do, waylaid by his own
story? The hand checks as the mouth goes dry — it will be
240   unable to cry for help in the nightmare version for which
these lines are the coming attraction!) The women loom in their doorways
and fall upon their sleeping husbands to hack and stab
the poor besotted heroes home at last from the war.
There were some, the prudent and sober, still in their armor, alert
to trouble, their minds clear and their torches still ablaze.
But what can they do? Fight? Flee? The goddess had made
the women huge, unearthly apparitions. They cower
as if before the combined Eumenides, as if
Bellona herself approached with her sword above their heads.
250   Thus were the women transformed, not only wives, but sisters,
and even the daughters and mothers: all were turned butchers now
and they dragged their men from their beds, whom Getic hordes had assailed
in vain, and Bessi attacked, and the rage of the stormy sea
tested and not found wanting. The bedchambers ran with blood

from bubbling wounds. The dying men rolled from their beds
like logs that fall from untended fires. Some women, meanwhile,
were torching their own roofs to reduce to anonymous ashes
those homes they had come to hate. Here and there, from the flames,
men appeared in the doorways to find that their way was barred
by unyielding wives with naked swords ready to strike,   260
at the sight of which they turned back to die in the conflagration.
There were groans and cries from the men and, from Thracian slaves, barbaric
curses . . . or were they perhaps their pleas of supplication?
   Against such a sordid background, how can I find the words
of praise for Hypsipyle's courage and virtue, the single exception,
that lone gleam of light in Lemnos' darkest hour?
Your name shall shine in my story, that the ages of men may recall it,
as long as the list of Roman dignitaries survives
for antiquaries to study, and as long as Latin is read.
The women had all gone mad, the daughters and wives of men   270
who were women's sons were crazed, possessed by their common madness,
and everywhere on the island in the garish light of the flames
were enacted, in scenes of private horror, unspeakable crimes.
But the good Hypsipyle has not lost her mind. She warns
her father, "Run away! Flee this city! I beg you,
and flee from me, as well." With her sword in her hand, she tells him,
"It is no enemy army, no Thracian horde at the walls.
This is what we have done ourselves. Do not inquire
who or why, but begone, while you still can get away.
I'm afraid my mind's not right. I beg you, take this sword   280
I hold in my hand and escape!" Supporting his frail limbs,
she covers his head and face and leads him away in silence
to Bacchus' holy shrine. Confiding there in the god,
she stretches forth her hands to pray, "Io! Bacchus, save me,
keep me from this sin and show me your pity and love."
Then she seats her father at the feet of the god's icon
and hides him in its flowing robes. At the break of dawn,
there are sounds of human voices and the tinkle of ritual cymbals,
and the lynxes at the temple gates greet the new day
roaring in their strength and vigor as Dawn in her car   290
climbs the bowl of the sky. This princess of Lemnos remarks
on the sudden stillness. The fit of violence seems to have passed.

Good deeds, they say, will inspire courage, and righteous actions
impart to the soul a firmness of purpose and noble assurance.
Thus it is with Hypsipyle. On her father's brow, she arrays
votive garlands of flowers and arranges his hair like a boy's.
She decks him in Bacchic robes and has him mount into a car
equipped with cymbals and drums and the rest of the ritual gear.
She dons the ivy herself, twining the sacred vines

300 around her bosom and arms, and takes up a vine-wrapped wand
with which to smite the air. She looks back at Thoas, her father,
wearing his ceremonial robes and grasping the reins,
to look persuasive to people who will think of the god as they see him
holding the goblet aloft and wearing the sacral horns
on his snowy hair. She opens the grating gates and ventures
into the streets, calling aloud, "O Bacchus, Bacchus,
abandon these bloodstained precincts. Let the sea come to cleanse
the pollution here of death. Let me bring your serpents
into your temple once more and consecrate them anew."

310 This was her way of traveling safe through the fearsome carnage,
for the god himself conspired, striking awe into hearts
of those who saw her, aglow, possessed, and divinely inspired.
She left the cruel city behind them and brought the old man
to the silent woods, where she hid him. Still, by day and night,
her fears persisted: her bold deed had cheated the Furies
of one of their victims. No longer could she join in the festival dances—
having tricked them once, she was frightened now to go back.
And she couldn't return to that woodland glen where she'd left her father,
whose escape was yet incomplete. How could she get him to safety?

320 She remembered a dinghy, a hulk on the beach that the savage sea
had reduced almost to wreckage, an offering, call it, to Thetis
and Glaucus. Time in the sun had baked it, and moonlight hoarfrost
worn it further away. To this poor vessel she took him,
in the dark of night, her father from out of the woods to the shingle
and there, in sorrow, she spoke: "What kind of country is this?
What kind of land are you leaving behind, despoiled of its manhood?
What a defilement! The ruin that one night worked its will
upon us all! I am forced to entrust you to this frail craft,
this ghost of a boat! But what is the choice? To keep you here

330 on this nightmare island? I thought I had been so clever, but this

is what it all comes down to. Hear my prayer, O goddess,
who drives that sleepy car over the darkling ocean.
I do not ask for a throne for my father, no subject people,
but only that he may escape from his home on his native island.
When shall I be able to share with my neighbors my joy
that my father's life has been spared? When will they come to their senses
and pour forth the bitter tears their wicked deeds should prompt?"
She cannot say any more. He shoves off in the boat
and floats away to reach the Tauri's land and Diana's
cult of runaway slaves where fugitives look for asylum.   340

   The daughter returns to the town and the citadel, where the women
have gathered together, a strange and unkempt group, distracted
and strident. The subject before them is how to govern the city,
what laws to enact and whom to appoint to the seat of power.
Hypsipyle is their choice. They give her her father's scepter,
as if by right (or the gods were rewarding a daughter's devotion).

   And now they see the vessel, the *Argo*, approaching Lemnos,
scudding along as the sunlight flashes on flailing oars.
The queen, of course, is concerned, and she calls her council together
to discuss what they should do. Prepare to attack the intruders?   350
But the passions Venus had stirred in their hearts, Vulcan now soothed,
while Polyxo, the foreign-born priestess Apollo once had loved,
declared that you, O Tethys, and Proteus set the course
that brought them to Lemnos' harbor as if a team of divine
seals had drawn them hither. (This seer was familiar with water,
was said, in fact, to submerge herself and bring back reports
from below the waves of the gods' intentions.) She argued now:
"Let us allow them to dock. Destiny brings them. Trust me,
the god that favors Lemnos has guided these visiting Minyae.
Venus herself has granted that we may mate with these sailors   360
and with our still-fertile wombs repopulate our island."
Her words are at once accepted, and Iphinoë carries the message
down to the shore to the Greeks, who do not seem offended
by the guilt of the women whose crimes have purged the place of males,
for Venus, Cythera's queen, has banished fear from their hearts.

· ·

And then he fells an enormous ox on behalf of the chiefs
and makes the sacrificial offerings in those rites

for which there had been no priests to serve, and he gives a heifer
to sizzle on Venus' altar, and the smoke ascends in her honor.

370   They arrived then at a crag where the overhanging rocks
and ridges were black with smoke and the air all around was heated.
Jason stopped, and the queen bade him pray and explained
that the place was holy: "The caverns of Vulcan are here within.
You must offer wine and blessings. In this cave are his lightning bolts
and the night may demonstrate these marvels, the roar of the furnace
and the loud clang on the anvil where the god forges the metal."
She shows him the fortified places, the island's strength and its wealth,
the heritage of their great forebears. At the palace, servants
prepare a sumptuous feast in the hall where the couches are covered
380   with Tyrian purple stuff. (These servants are Thracian women
in mourning still for their husbands who had never in fact profaned,
as their mistresses all supposed, the Lemnian marriage beds.)
At the place of honor is Jason, and next to him the queen,
and they take their seats in the hall with the other valiant captains.
Their appetite is robust for the flesh of the sacrificial
beasts as they pass the wine in the ornamental cups,
and the hall is hushed in prayer. Then the banquet begins.
They while away the evening with food and conversation
and Hypsipyle asks Jason what destiny had drawn him
390   here and what were the sailing orders his king had given,
and how and where his ship was built, and she hangs on his words
and gazes at him, feeling the fires of passion warm her.
She gives herself to the pleasant prospect of giving herself.
The gods themselves conspire, for heaven's law had decreed
at this time of year when the Pleiades set below the horizon
storms descend on the earth and roil the seas as rain
sluices down from the sky and mountains are drenched and forests.
This is the season when fear grips the hearts of men,
for then Astrea, the goddess of justice, urges Jove
400   to visit upon the nations his punishment for their crimes,
and invoking Saturn's star for further aid, she implores
Southwest Wind and his brothers to rage on the turbulent seas
till the terrified waves fling themselves on the beach for refuge.
Tiphys, the *Argo*'s helmsman, notes how the rising moon
for the fourth time in a row is misted, and all the Minyae

agree that the risks are excessive. Their mission is best postponed
to the storm's relenting. Meanwhile, the city offers diversions,
the delights of connubial beds. They can spend their days and nights
living the sweet life. Their seafaring days will come,
but not just yet. The winds' crooning is not for them,   410
but Hercules, the Tiryns hero, down at the ship
where he has been keeping watch and avoiding the town's temptations,
is eloquent still. The gods, he insists, have not decreed
that his comrades have left their homes with the prayers of all their kinfolk
to settle for sybaritic days and erotic nights.
Is this what mighty Hercules ought to be doing, abetting
his shipmates' strenuous beddings? "For this have I signed on?
Give me Phasis, Aeëtes, the perils of Scythian seas.
Give me challenge, adventure, but not this inanition.
I came for the love of danger. You toy with the dangers of love.   420
My heart is set on the perils of the clashing Symplegades' rocks
and the rage of mythical monsters. Telamon here, and I,
are yours to command, but only if you will assume command."
Hearing his just complaint, Jason was filled with chagrin.
Like a warhorse that takes its ease in a peaceful nation's pasture,
he had gone sleek and sluggish, but his heart was not yet tamed,
and a part of him wished still for the bit in his teeth and the fierce
rider up in the saddle, the blare of the battle horn,
and the cries of fury and anguish he pricked his ears to hear.
Argus and Tiphys he calls, and bids them prepare the ship,   430
mustering all the men, putting the gear in order,
and gathering up the oars that lay there strewn on the beach.
    Now is the city again a scene of grief and mourning;
on every face is written the woe of being abandoned.
Who shall rule the island and wield the scepter? The women
will bear their children to absent fathers. The hopes they had raised
were dashed again. They had opened their hearts for a moment, assumed
the cares of marriage . . . But now the men were sailing away.
Even Hypsipyle, seeing that Jason was bound to leave,
groaned aloud in the useless complaint she addressed to her lover.   440
"Is our time together ended? At tomorrow's dawn, do you sail?
I loved you more than I loved my own father, but you
dallied here less for me than to wait out the weather. Eager,

as if the winds had held your ship on the desolate shore
of Thrace, you cannot wait to put to sea." She wept
and handed him her parting gift, a woven tunic
with needlework scenes depicting her father in that car
in which she'd contrived his rescue. Around him a fearful throng
makes way. And then in the next panel, he hides in the bosky
450 forest glen in the noontime shade. But a leap of faith
was now required, or at least some ground that improbable prayers
are sometimes granted. She showed the scene on leafy Ida
where Ganymede on an eagle's back rode up to heaven
to serve as Jove's cupbearer — stranger than even her father's
translation in that wretched shell of a boat. And she gave
Jason her father's sword and said, "In the thick of battle,
I shall be with you always, with this sword that Aetna's god
gave Thoas and I in turn have presented to you who are worthy
to bear this splendid weapon. Go, but do not forget
460 this peaceful land and its welcome into the warmth of my bosom.
Come back safe from Colchis' conquered shore to greet
your son, this new Jason you leave here in my womb."
Thus she spoke and clung to the neck of her husband, as did
the others, Orpheus' woman, and those of Peleus, Castor,
and Pollux, all of them weeping. Meanwhile the anchor is raised
from the clinging embrace of the sand. They push off, and oars are flailing
and the breeze picks up and their wake is a widening pathway of foam.
Lemnos shrinks behind, and, before them, Electra's island,
Samothrace, is looming larger, the home of the cult
470 of the Thracian rites, for here the terrible deities dwell,
the Cabiri, but no one may write of this cult without the risk
of their curses. Jove himself protects these shores with his fierce
waves that break on the dangerous beach to discourage sailors.
But Thyotes the priest comes down to the shore to greet the Minyae
and welcome them to the island. He guides them through the temples,
the mysteries of which he explains to his guests, but the poet,
out of respect and reverence, must omit these from his tale.

Filled now with heavenly visions, the Minyae back at their thwarts
were on their way. First Imbros slid by, ahead, abeam,
480 and then astern, as the sun rose up and then sank in the sky.
Then, for the first time since the world began, a ship

from Thessaly's shores drew up at fate's bidding at Troy,
where, on the beach at Sigeum, the men leapt ashore. Forthwith,
using their sails as tents, they pitched their camp, ground meal,
and with sparks struck from their flints set cookfires blazing.
    Walking along the shore, Hercules and his friend
Telamon heard sounds . . . The waves or a human voice
murmuring in its sadness? They could see nothing and no one,
but heard it yet, distinctly, and attempted to track it down.
A woman's voice? A girl's! She was calling out to the gods   490
and men to come and help her, desperate and left to perish
in a most cruel death. The heroes resolved to try.
Tumult, then, and rage, as if, in some wild defile,
a bull roared in its pain from a lion riding its back
and mauling its flesh with its teeth and cruel claws, while herdsmen
look on in distress and amazement. Hercules peered up the cliff
and spied on the crest of a crag the sorry face of the maiden
shackled there and crying in understandable terror,
the perfect picture of woe some craftsman might have inscribed
on an ivory plaque or painted on clear Parian marble.   500
But the maiden was all too real, and Hercules spoke up:
"Who in the world are you? What is your family? How
did you come to this sad plight? Who put those bonds on your wrists
at which you strain your slender arms?" With her eyes cast down
and her voice a quaver of grief and shame, she answered the hero:
"I am guiltless and have not deserved this torment. You see
the rich stuffs of purple and gold with which these rocks
are bizarrely bedecked? My parents' last gifts to their daughter!
Our line goes back to noble Ilus, and, happy once,
we ruled these lands in peace until Fortune turned her back   510
on Laomedon's house. A plague came down, a kind of miasma
from the blue sky into which the smoke from pyres wreathed
together to stain the air, and then came an earthquake and waves
of enormous size from the sea. The woods on Ida's flanks
shuddered in fear, and then, from the ocean, a monster emerged
of vast bulk, a mountain of beastly flesh, a terror
beyond all measure or calculation. To this, every year,
a band of maidens is chosen as sacrificial victims
as the horned priests of Ammon have ordered: a virgin's life

520 must be offered up and her body given to his desire.
I am the one unlucky enough to have drawn the lot
that condemns me to these rocks. But if prayers are ever answered
and heaven again should listen to Phrygian supplications,
if you are the savior omens have promised and I have imagined,
know my father is now feeding the snow-white horses
he has sworn to give as reward to one who would save his daughter
and deliver Troy from this curse. You must be that man.
Not even when gods labored together to build the walls
of Troy that reach to the skies have I seen so broad a chest,
530 such arms, such mighty shoulders." She looked about her forlornly
at the bleak shore beneath the leaden clouds into which
those pyres still poured smoke. A landscape out of a nightmare,
the hero thought, the like of which he had seen before
on the way to the Nemean woods or on Erymanthus' slopes
or at Lerna's noxious marshland where he slew the dreaded Hydra.

In the distance, at Neptune's signal, the monster produced a roar
from its home in the depths of the gulf, and the waters of Troy were roiled
by its sinister thrashing, the waves crashing on shore. In the spray
one could make out the shape of its head and its eyes, which flashed
540 fire. A stertorous bellow arose from its cavernous maw,
and its teeth gleamed in menace as it coiled and then uncoiled,
dragging its grotesque length along in the rocky shallows
while seawater sluiced from the scales of its flanks. One could not say
if it were the cause or result of this turbulence. Less fiercely
do tempests rage that South Wind visits upon the sea,
or even Orion's gales when he grasps his father's reins
tightly and whips his team of horses into a frenzy.
Telamon stood there in shock as his friend seemed to grow larger
to meet this threat, to match its fury with that of his own
550 spirit and mighty body, huge in its shining armor
with that quiver loaded with rattling arrows that bounced on his back.
With a prayer to Jove, his father, and all the gods of the sea
and a blessing on his weapons he leapt up to a rock,
looked down at the shuddering water stirred to its depths,
and appraised the dragon's coils and the spume of the sea it produced
as it thrashed and whipped the waves. So North Wind, when it rises
out of the Hebrus' ravines, flings great clouds through the sky

that obscure the Arcadian mountains. The beast in the water reared
its awesome bulk and its back rose up as big as a mountain
but one that moved, approaching. Its shadow spread on the beach,   560
and, inland, Ida trembled as if it had been assaulted
by another intruding mountain that threatened to break it apart.
Hercules grabbed his bow and let fly a storm of arrows
but to no more effect than the rain when it tries to melt Mount Eryx
and wash it away. The monster was coming fast, and arrows
were awkward now and useless. For the first time, Hercules doubts
and wonders what madness prompted him to this foolhardy
and ruinous undertaking. The maiden's shame and fear
he begins to feel, himself. He looks around for a missile,
a boulder perhaps . . . He sees great stones the surf has dislodged   570
from the base of the cliff, but now the monster is closing upon him,
coiling its terrible coils as it writhes along on its belly,
its dreadful jaws agape. Hip deep in the surf
Hercules stands his ground, ready, awaiting his chance,
and then, as the monster's head descends, he strikes with a rock
shattering blows at the side of the neck and then, with his huge
club, bone-crushing blows at the base of the animal's skull,
again and again, and the beast sinks down into the sea
and its coiled body goes slack, and it floats, dead weight in the water.

    The queen of Troy is weeping in gratitude and relief.   580
Her attendants are sobbing with her, still feeling the fear
and grief from which they are now spared by the hero's deed.
From the hills, the joyful shepherds make their way to the city,
having heard reports of what has come to pass. Meanwhile,
Telamon returns to the ship to explain to his comrades
why the water on which they sail has turned blood red,
and Hercules climbs the cliff to reach the fettered maiden
and untie the cruel bonds of her hands and feet to the rock.
Then he adjusts his armor and is ready to march in triumph
to meet the king. He is like a bull who has frightened away   590
a pack of wolves and prances back to the pasture, his head
high on his muscular shoulders to inspect the herd he has saved.

    The Phrygians come to greet him, a happy throng released
from the long night of their torment. Laomedon leads the procession
with his loving wife at his side and his son, the baby Priam.

He has his daughter back but is less than delighted, for now
the horses he prizes are claimed as the hero's rightful reward.
The populace, ecstatic, crowds into the city streets
and climbs the walls to catch a glimpse of their splendid savior,
600   but the king's face is grim, a deceitful mask when he speaks
of a father's love and a king's great debt: "O bravest of Greeks,
it was pure chance that brought you here to Troy. You did not
come in pity for us, or even know of our plight.
If the stories men tell are true and Jove is indeed your father,
you are then of our blood, for Jove is our forebear, too.
On this shore so distant from home, you are yet among your kinsmen,
and after our many tears, we greet you in joy, delighted
that you have come, and only wish that it had been sooner.
But here you are, and welcome. Call your comrades to join us
610   within these walls and tomorrow, at first light, we will show you
the horses your deed has won." He ceased to speak, but his mind
raced to contrive some way by which he might yet avoid
giving those steeds to the stranger. Kill him at night in his bed,
using perhaps those deadly arrows the oracle said
would first bring ruin to Troy and then its utter destruction?
But who can change the decrees of the Fates, who have written down
how the Greeks one bloody night will plunder the conquered city
from which disaster Aeneas will flee to found a new
and grander Troy? The hero of Tiryns explains to the king
620   that he and his companions are bound for the Scythian seas,
"but we shall soon return to your shores," he says, "and then
shall I claim that rich reward you have promised." In answer, the king
swears up and down to keep his word and pay his debt,
but his Phrygian subjects, who know him, weep to hear these oaths
they are sure he means to break, and they dread the divine wrath
such treacherous dealings must call down on king and unfortunate kingdom.

The ship is again under sail and Ilium's shores glide by,
the tombs of their ancient kings and the lively people at play
in their festive games. Behind them, on Ida's flank, one can see
630   the fires lit for the rites of sacrifice, and Gargara
resounds with the music of flutes that the breezes carry to seaward.
But they fade away into silence as the ship makes its way through the straits.
At dawn, with a following wind, they are flying along when the waves

open and Helle appears, a sea goddess now, a sister
of Panope and Thetis. She wears on her head a wreath
and holds in her hand a scepter of gold with which she lulls
the heaving waves. Jason she then addresses with gentle
words: "You, too, are driven from Greece across strange seas
by inimical men at home and a destiny hard as my own.
Fortune is frowning again on Aeolus' offspring to bring you   640
to the Scythian coast where a vast land meets a measureless sea.
Be bold and do not falter. Far off is the mouth of the River
Phasis and it will admit you. But stop, for there is a glade
hidden away, with twin altars of piled-up turf,
where you must offer the proper prayers to my brother Phrixus,
and convey to his poor dust these words with which I entrust you:
'Brother, I do not wander among the shades on the shore
of the dismal Styx. Do not, my dear one, search for me there
in Avernus' caverns and do not fret that my corpse may be tossed
by the waves on the cruel rocks of the sea. As soon as I fell,   650
Cymothoë and Glaucus came at once to my aid with a kindly
welcome to me for my pains to this new abode in the sea god's
rich realm. Our gulf is a pleasant place, a match
for Ino's tranquil sea.'" She then fell silent, thinking
of the grief of her poor father at the loss of both his children,
and concealed her sorrowing face beneath the water's surface.
Jason then poured wine on the sea and addressed her, "Cretheus'
daughter, you are a sea goddess now, and I invoke
your aid to a kinsman's perilous voyage and bold adventure."

        The ship sailed on through the Dardanelles, with Europe's cliffs   660
on the one side and, on the other, Asia's gentler slopes.
These lands were connected once and their peoples lived together,
but over the eons the force of the thrashing ocean tore them
apart, as in ancient times they sundered Sicily's coast
and cut it off from the mainland, or Atlas and Janus struggled
to tear with a mighty roar Gibraltar from Africa's coast.
The ridges of Percote they passed and Parium's treacherous shoals,
and Pitya and then Lampsacus dwindled away astern.
(Lampsacus is where they worship Priapus in sordid rites
one hesitates to imagine. The Minyae could make out his image,   670
crudely ithyphallic, carved on their buildings and shrines.)

They were out of the straits now, and the bowl of the sea and sky
opened wide before them to show them a whole new world.

    Halfway down the Propontus, a sand spit that kept on growing,
a peninsula, juts out into the sea connected
by a narrow and very defensible neck of land to the coast.
There was the city of Cyzicus, a rich and prosperous king,
and beyond the shallows one could admire its fertile fields
and then the walls of the town. That king, hearing reports
680   of the Greek ship, came down himself to the water's edge
to behold this marvel and greet these heroes from far away.
He clasped their hands in warm welcome and friendship and said,
"You men of Greece are strangers to us, as we are to you,
but distance is not difference. Now that you've found the way,
we may rejoice together in what can unite mankind.
There are savage people here in this harsh terrain, and a sea
·that thunders around us in menace, but we are by no means brutes.
Loyalty one can find here, and honor, much like your own,
and the worship of gods, and the kindness of man to his fellow men.
690   We are not like the Bebryces beyond us along the coast,
or the Scythians with their cruel frenzies and savage rites."
Having said this, he ushers his guests into the town
and orders the doors be opened in friendship to them. In the temples
are services of thanksgiving. In the palace banquet hall,
bejeweled and gilded couches await the festive meal
where a hundred youths will serve the meat and pour the wine
into ceremonial beakers engraved with battle scenes
Cyzicus is eager to gloss for his noble guests:
"Here is the enemy's sneak attack on our harbor at night,
700   and here you see them flee, the Pelasgians, on their rafts
we have just set ablaze!" To this Aeson's son replies,
"If only they might come tonight in another rash
attempt, what could we not do together, your men and mine?
You'd never have to worry again!" And they joked, told stories,
and talked throughout the night and most of the following day.

Book III

For the third time Tithonus' bride dispelled the clammy
shadows of night and opened the curtains of morning. The calm
of the blue ocean that promised an easy voyage called out
to Tiphys, who summoned the crew of the *Argo* to march from the palace
down to the shore along with the friendly Cyzican townsmen,
who gave them the best sheep of their flocks and grain and wine—
not the cheap Bithnyian kind, or Phrygian plonk, but rich,
the wonderful cuvé from the Lesbian grapes that grow
along the Straits of Helle. Cyzicus, arm in arm
with Jason as they walk to the shore, weeps at their parting   10
and gives him princely gifts: a robe embroidered with golden
thread his wife, Clite, had given him; also a helmet
and invincible spear his father had borne in battle. The king
in turn receives from Jason a goblet and splendid bridle
Thessalian craftsmen had fashioned. They clasp hands as they swear
a friendship as close as kinship, as if their houses were one.
　　O, Clio, my muse, speak now through me to disclose the sad
and all but unspeakable denouement. You know the hearts
and minds of the gods and can fathom their strange behavior toward men.
How could Jove have allowed these heroes' hands that had clasped   20
in amity then to be raised against one another in battle?
Where in the score does it say that a clarion's blast must resound,
and why should the Erinys trouble the peace of this tranquil city?
　　We must go back in time to one of King Cyzicus' raids
on Dindymus, with its temples to the Phrygians' mother goddess,
Cybele, where the people run through the woods with their arms

bloodied from cuts they inflict on themselves in their ecstasy. There,
riding his battle car, the king gave chase once to a lion
he managed to slay with a well-aimed javelin throw, not knowing
30 that this was a sacred beast, one of the goddess' team
that drew her chariot. He, having no idea, returned
with its head and mane as a trophy, an occasion more for shame
than for any possible glory. And now, the resentful goddess
nursing her grudge beholds from her mountain fastness where cymbals'
music floats on the air that ship making its way
with the kingly shields arrayed on the gunwales to port and starboard
and she seizes upon this chance to visit the heartbreaking horror
she has only vaguely imagined — those friends in mortal combat
enmeshed in their misapprehension and the toils of her wicked devising.

40   Night, but the starlit spray at the prow and the transom's wake
sparkled fluorescent white as the ship slipped along on the gentle
sea with a following wind bearing it on. Her oars
were shipped and the men were mostly dozing. The course was set
for the isle of Marmora, beyond the mouth of the River Rhyndacus,
which spills its silt and stains the sea a blue-green brown
well beyond sight of the shore. Scylaceum's promontory
where the waves break into foam would have been next, but the pilot's
eyes that should have been staring out to the stars and the shore
were drooping, as Sleep, at the bidding of gods and goddesses, touched him,
50 making his eyelids heavy as never before and soothing
all shadow of care from his mind. His head nods and his hand
slips from the smooth tiller. The ship is the winds' plaything
and they nudge it this way and that, and turn it around on a heading
back to that friendly harbor from which it has just put out.

    As it was approaching the channel it had left not long before,
trumpets blared an alarm and a watchman's voice cried out
a warning of a sneak attack: "The Pelasgian foe is upon us."
Groggy, roused from their beds, the city's fighters hurried
this way and that through the streets where Pan, Lord of the Woodlands
60 and Master of War, had spread his confusion and panic. In daylight
he lurks in his caves to emerge at night, shaggy and wreathed,
Cybele's son, to stir the blood or chill the hearts
of men of war. At his hoarse shouts, louder than cornets'
blasts, brave men dropped swords and skillful charioteers

were toppled out of their cars. Disorder governs the moment:
the bolts of the city gates fall open. (Or had they been closed?)
Terror, greater even than that which comes from the awful
helmet of Mars or the wild hair of the Furies and Gorgons,
seizes the town as phantoms and monsters loom and dissolve,
and the god laughs at the scene where men stampede like cattle,   70
like flocks and herds that break from their pens to flatten the brush.

    Then Cyzicus hears the racket that wakes him from troubling dreams
to real disaster, for there at the windows and doorways, Bellona's
dread presence looms, her bronze accouterments clanking
in ruinous omen, the black plumes on her helmet waving
to show the ill wind's motion. She smites the rooftree and summons
the distracted king, who follows along to the city walls
to command the fight he is all but certain will be his last.
Think of Rhoetus, the Centaur, drunk at that fight with the Lapiths,
attempting to squint the world into focus and knowing he's doomed   80
as he rushes at Theseus, desperate but seeing no choice or escape;
or think of Athamas, maddened by Juno, home from the hunt,
with the corpse of his son, Learchus, over his shoulder like game
he's bagged, while Thebes looks away in horror, grief, and disgust:
such is Cyzicus' desperate case as, from gate to gate,
he runs while the men of the watch, following close at his heels,
hear on all sides from house to house the tumult and shouting.

    For their part, the Minyae are struck with dread and their sick hearts
quail, for they cannot tell where they are or whom to fear
or from where in the darkness a helmet or shield may glint, or from what   90
direction a sharp spear at any moment may fly.
And then they hear the peculiar rush and the sickening thud
as the spearpoint they have imagined materializes to strike
the strakes of the hull, and the crew snatches up their weapons.
Jason, donning his helmet, prays aloud, "O father,
this is your son's first battle," and then, to the men, says "Courage!
This, my friends, is that first encounter for which we have longed
with the forces of Colchis." As Mars' chariot swoops from its course
among the stars to the midst of his Thracian heirs, the Bistones,
and the shouting of bloodthirsty men and blare of the brazen trumpets   100
fills the heart of the god with delight, so he is pleased
now with the men on this ground as Achaean fighters swarm

ashore following Jason, close their ranks, and advance
together in grim phalanx that the goddess herself could not
dismay with her breast's aegis clanging upon her armor,
nor Fear and Dread, the horses of Mars, make turn and run.
Their shields are knit together as they bear down on the town
like a thunderhead that the winds advance in a darkening menace
that men who watch it cannot hope to flee . . . Which way?
110   They are torn between fear and the thought that there may be some escape.
Will the storm strike them or perhaps relent and head out to sea?
    The unhappy band of Cyzicans shout, fling stones, and hurl
burning brands. They whirl their slingshots, but no reaction
comes from the Greeks who endure or, indeed, ignore these displays.
Mopsus watched, and Eurytus, as Corythus, large in his armor,
advancing toward them, stopped midstride, repelled by the bright
sheen of their massed weapons, like a shepherd who comes to a brook
the rains have fed where the water rages, and has to draw back
and watch the hurtling tree trunks its eddies hurry along.
120   Tydeus hailed him and taunted, "You! Die where you stand!
I was stronger once, and younger, but I'm more than enough for you,
face to face, this way, as you see me now!" And then
he threw his lance and pierced the Cyzican man in the groin,
and he groaned and fell and his teeth bit down on the dirt as the spasms
of anguish expelled the lance point in a gush of crimson blood.
Imagine a jagged rock that lurks in the sea, and unlucky
helmsmen hit it and wreck their vessels and drown. Just so
the Cyzican troops rushed blindly, their swords in their hands, and fell,
Iron first, and Cotys, and Bienor, Pyrnus' son.
130   Elsewhere, throughout the city, there is noise and great confusion.
Genysus' wife had thought to fetch him his weapons, and he,
armed but without his sword, had seized instead a brand
from the hearth fire, while Medon, late at the banquet table
still spread with its food, and the rites not yet performed, rushed out
in his festive robes, not looking warlike at all except
for the sword in his hand. These two, a contrast in martial fashion
and at opposite ends of town, yet meet identical fates,
for both are slain that night. And here comes Phlegyas, running
toward the invaders and waving a torch with its pitch blazing.
140   He assumes it's another raid, a band of Pelasgian villains

who like to hit and run and are lightly armed, and shouts
a challenge to one and all and plants himself near the harbor,
huge as Typhon himself when he glares down from the sky
red with fire and storm clouds, while Jove, in heaven, holds him
fast by his long hair. But rushing upon him, his bow
already bent, is the hero of Tiryns, who aims for the torch,
or just below it, and lets an arrow fly, unerring,
that pierces Phlegyas' chest, and he pitches forward to fall
with his face on the torch, and his beard catches fire and feeds the flame.
Peleus then dispatches Ambrosius; valiant Ancaeus   150
kills the brave Echeclus and then turns around to face
Telecoön coming up behind him: he swings his axe
left, then right, and detaches the skull from the bleeding neck.
He notices glints of light on the dead man's fancy corselet
and kneels to strip the corpse of this trophy, but Nestor sees him
and tells him, "Leave it. The sharp blade that is in your hand
is the only precious metal you need at the present moment."
Ancaeus looks up to watch his companion seize Amastrus,
prune the head from his body, and then call out to his comrades
that their foe is now in retreat and they should advance and pursue.   160
They break from their phalanx and leave the line of their shields to rove
for whomever they find in the darkness scattering this way and that.
Phlias, big as a building, comes upon Ochus, while Pollux
falls upon quivering Hebrus. Jason, the lord of the field
and the battle's master, appears to hover over the bodies,
splashed in blood and gore, a force of nature, a storm
whipping the waves of the killing. Zelys he wounds, and Brontes,
and Abaris, too, and he leaves them dying if not yet dead
to catch up with Glaucus. He does, and Glaucus falls as he deals him
a mortal blow that gashes his throat, and Glaucus grabs   170
the javelin shaft and gurgles some incomprehensible words
before the weapon sinks deeper, and then the man is silent.
Jason moves on and cuts down Halys with one great slash
of his sharp sword, then Protis, and Dorceus, famous for singing,
said to be second in skill with the lyre to Orpheus only.
Hercules, meanwhile, has abandoned quiver and bow
and now, with his huge club, flails about him with blows
like those of a woodsman's axe, and the heavy oaks and pines

of the forest creak, groan, and then crash as the wedges are driven
180 home into the hearts of the trees. So men now fall,
the bones of warriors crashing on hard ground and their brains
scattering white on the earth. Nimble Admon is stilled,
Hercules having seized his chin strap and beard and fetched him
a lethal blow from above. "Die, and be proud that the club
of Hercules has killed you!" is what he shouts, and the other
shudders as he falls down, stunned to hear his killer's
name, which is that of his friend. This burden he carries with him
into the land of the shades. A dark hour, Oryntus,
and nothing could help or evade or diminish the pain. You had greeted
190 Thessaly's princes in friendship, implored them to lengthen their stay,
and offered prayers of thanksgiving to your household gods for the honor
of knowing these men. But Idmon approaches and, wearing the helmet
you had given him, richly worked, with a scarlet plume,
it's he who strikes you the blow that ends your life. And you,
Crenaeus, how can one look at your wretched plight as your youth
and strength ooze out on the ground and sleep's oblivion dulls
those eyes of yours that had flashed so bright with the zest of life?
No more shall you rove in the woods or flirt on the shore with sea nymphs.
Elsewhere on the field was Sages fighting to good effect
200 when Hylas, the youthful member of Jason's crew, undid him
(a promising lad, that Hylas, and he would, if only the Fates
and Juno had been less cruel, have turned out as one of the *Argo*'s
greatest fighters). He shot an arrow that pierced the man's
heart. Then, in the melee, come by chance together
the twin sons of Tyndarus, Castor and Pollux, each
ready to strike the other, but just in time, on the brows
of each a glint from a torch or some inner radiance shone,
and they recognized one another, checked themselves, and drew back.
Castor then pierced Itys at the sword belt he wore at his waist
210 worked with the figures of serpents whose bite at last he felt,
while Pollux hacked at Hages, and Thapsus, and, right behind him,
Neacles, who brandished an axe. Then he hit Cydrus,
his face pale from the loss of blood from Canthus' wound.
At last, with all his strength, he hurled his spear through the air
at Erymus, the hunter, but a glint of moonlight showed
the intended victim the shaft of the weapon, as if in pity

the goddess felt for her devotee, who moved his head
just enough so the spear parted the plume on his helmet
and its sharp point struck the metal crest with a clang
and bounced to the ground harmless. Telamon struck Nisaeus   220
and then with his spear pierced the wickerwork shield of Opheltes,
that vain and boastful man, and the point went into his belly.
Telamon cried out in triumph, "O heaven, or luck, let it be
a king or a prince of noble blood or great repute,
for whom the city will mourn in general lamentation!"
Ares he killed, and his brother Melanthus, and Phocus, Olenus'
son, who had come from the Leleges' land, an exile, whose talent
and charm had earned him a place as attendant and friend in the court.
It is midnight, but loud with shouting and thick with the stench of blood
as the bodies pile up. You'd think you were out somewhere on an island,   230
Inarime, for instance, that trembles, about to erupt,
or Vesuvius even, when roused to strike fear in the cities
along its flank, and the smoke from its crater blots out the starlight
to deepen the darkness of Night as she crosses the sky in her car.

    Ah, my Muse, now help me with this tale of that nightmare battle.
Phaethon's dreadful progress, which wicked Tisiphone loved,
was such a dawning, for daylight revealed a scene of disaster
beyond all imagination. Banners were dropped on the ground
here and there among corpses the Furies had gathered that night,
the harvest of those sharp weapons, and earth was warm from the blood   240
those heroes had spilled, and their ghosts still fled from the Minyae's pursuit.
Cyzicus, in his confusion, rushes about, exultant,
supposing his army has triumphed and put the invaders to flight,
for no Pelasgian raiders are still on the field. The gods
are cruel and sometimes toy with men in their moment of ruin.
Think of Coeus, the Titan, in Tartarus' pit, and his desperate
schemes as he breaks the chains in which Jove has bound him, and rises
invoking Saturn and calling out to enormous Tityus
for help in another vain attempt to scale the walls
of heaven's fortress. So, pathetic, Cyzicus rages   250
and shouts his boasts and taunts and he roams the field and summons
his troops to join in the fight: "Your king calls you! Respond,
as if to your priest's command and Cybele's savage pipes
and similar holy objects, and join in this orgy of killing.

Feel the heat of the blood of our victims that streams down our arms."
But the goddess' madness abates and a chill seizes his heart
as he looks around and listens. He hears, like a roar of lions,
the blare of battle trumpets and sees large shapes in the darkness
approaching, and then he feels the heavy spear of their chief
260   as Jason's javelin hits him and strikes him close to the heart.
A sharp pang of remorse he also feels, a regret
for the pains of those woodland beasts he has slain himself with his spear.
So do the great-souled heroes hurl their spears in an eddying
whirlwind of death and pursue this way and that the footfalls
of possible foes. They seize their comrades-in-arms from whom
they demand the day's watchword. It could have gone on all night,
in which case dawn would have broken upon utter ruin, the race
destroyed at last, with only mothers, bereft, looking down
from the city walls to their sons' corpses strewn on the shingle.
270   But then, in his mercy, the Father of Heaven, omnipotent, stopped it:
their king was dead. Enough. He broke off the wretched fighting,
and brought relief at last, nodding his august head
at which the children of Night and the War God tremble in fear.
He closes the gate of war, and men in disorder flee
the gory field, and the Minyae relent as their bloodlust ebbs,
giving way at last to reason, reflection, and even doubt
as dawn scatters the first faint rays of the day's new light
from the harbor and turreted walls of the town to the scenes of its horror.
In the midst of the ranks, Tiphys exclaims, "O gods of the sea,
280   what have you done? What ruin has followed upon my dozing?
I nodded off to wake to a nightmare my comrades lived through,
destroying this friendly shore." His shipmates are speechless, frozen
in dread at what they have done and, silent, they bind their wounds.
At the end of the Bacchanal, when the god withdrew his frenzy
and the women's spirits no longer were seized, they must have looked down
at Pentheus' torn body and felt such shame and chagrin
when the drums' and horns' shrill music had faded away to a silence
awful to have to bear. On the other side, the townsmen,
the women and men too old to fight, are appalled to discover
290   the carnage these men who were friends have inflicted upon their loved ones,
and they turn to flee, but Jason holds out his hand and calls:
"From whom do you run? I wish that we were the ones who had fallen.

This is not what I wanted but the work of some cruel god
who used us thus for a purpose that wasn't in any way ours.
We are the Minyae! These are our friends and sworn allies!
Let us do what we must to prepare the funeral honors."

The mourners swarm over the field and its piles of corpses,
searching for clues they fear to find: a mother stops
as she recognizes a piece of fabric she wove herself,
or a wife, staring down at the ground, weeps to see the gift   300
she gave the broken body that has to be her husband's.
Along the desolate shoreline, the wails ascend to the skies
and from here and there are groans and bubbling noises the dying
make at the last, and with trembling hands the servants and mothers
close their eyelids. And then, in the midst of the heap of the dead,
they find the king's pale body, and a shriller keening is heard
so loud as to drown out the rest of the moaning and lamentation.
Here the mourners assemble to grieve, and the weeping Minyae
are sick to their souls and keening in grief for their terrible deed
and that fatal stroke of Jason's spear. They console their captain,   310
who looks down at the ashen cheeks and the hair matted
with clotted gore and can scarcely recognize the face
of the man who, the day before, had been his host and friend.
Clasping the lifeless limbs, he cries aloud, "Poor man,
but at least you are secure in the clutches of night and spared
the bitter pangs of remorse I feel, the shame and blame
with which I am heavily burdened here in the light of the living.
What a bitter meeting this is, the grotesque reunion that Fortune
has engineered! That I should have raised my hand against you . . .
Who could have ever imagined my destiny might include   320
so dreadful a thing? But that was our doom and the gods had willed it.
Alas! Had their plan been just, I should be lying dead
and you would be standing here and grieving over my corpse.
One might have supposed the prophets and seers to whom the gods
have given the gift and who spoke of the death of my agèd father
and other woes as well might have thought fit to mention
that this bizarre disaster awaited us both. I am cursed.
Where now can I go? What welcome may I now expect
from others who soon will have heard that this is how I behave
to a host and friend? I had hoped to return here from distant Phasis   330

and, having survived those trials and with Scythian wealth in my hold,
I'd visit here again, to rejoice and fight by your side
against your foes. That dream is dashed, but still may I press
my cheek to your lifeless cheek and my breast to your cold breast
in a last embrace. Come, men, roll down the funereal tree trunks
here to the shore for the pyres of these our comrades in arms
to whom we owe such honors as Cyzicus would have paid us."

    For her part, Clite, the widow, her hair streaming down on the face
of the dead man, calls out to the weeping women to wail
340   and share her grief: "O husband, taken from me in your prime,
you take my life with you. No children have I, no joys
with which to endure this blow of fate. O noblest man,
I am cheated of that small solace I might have had to assuage
these scalding tears. Of my father's love and my childhood home
Mygdonia's cruel army robbed me; my mother's tender
care Artemis' arrow brought to a sudden end.
You were together my husband, brother, parent, and child
and now are mine no more. Abandoned, alone, I am smitten
by heaven's heavy blows that have rained down on our city.
350   Ah, Cyzicus, you left me without any deathbed farewell
or last word of advice or affection or silent embrace
of the kind bereft widows remember in love and grief.
In our chamber, I waited for you to come back to me; now I behold
what is left to me of a husband — beyond all imagination."

    Now in teams, the shipmates strip trees from the hills for the pyres
on which to burn the bodies. Sadly they lay them out
on the piles of wood to which they lead the slain men's horses
and coursing hounds to be offered as gifts to their departed
masters' spirits. There, in the center and place of honor,
360   is the king's pyre at which the son of Aeson, weeping
in racking sobs, lifts up the corpse of his friend to place it
on a bier bedecked in royal purple. In tribute, he offers
a robe embroidered with threads of gold on the purple cloth
Hypsipyle of Lemnos had woven on her own loom
and given to Jason when he and his men were about to depart.
He also put on the pyre Cyzicus' elegant helmet
and the sword belt he had worn and, turning his face to the city,
he raised up the dead man's scepter that he had received from his forebears

but to which there was now no heir, for he was the last of his line.
This, too, Jason placed on the pyre so that the king   370
might bring it to those ancestors waiting to welcome his spirit.
Three times the pyres trembled as the Minyae marched around them
with heavy tread to the blare of the trumpets' baleful notes,
and then, with a farewell shout, they flung the burning torches
onto the readied tinder. The piled-up logs caught fire
that the winds whipped, and the dark water reflected the flames.
This was the fate that had long awaited the king and his people
from the time that the trees first grew on Pelion's slope, that the birds
of omen had long proclaimed, for those who knew how to read them,
writing upon the sky what thunderbolts would come.   380
But even when fate may be declared, who does not try
to evade or temporize or deny or disbelieve,
or hope for some reprieve? The ashes upon the beach
having had their proper honors are cooling now, and the wives
and children depart, and the waters, no longer stirred by laments,
are quieter now in the harbor, as when, in the spring, the birds,
quitting their winter quarters and migrating north from Egypt,
leave behind on the sunbaked Nile an eerie hush.

    All day and night, the Minyae bathe in the depths of their grief
as they see in their minds' eyes the faces of those who are dead.   390
The wind whips in the rigging and bids fair to belly the sails,
but the tide of their hearts' sorrow is still running strong, and they wait,
pouring forth more tears for those they have killed. Their homeland
forgotten, and their keen love of adventure all but extinguished,
they give themselves over to mourning and the sweet languor of woe.
Even Aeson's son, who as chief must maintain morale
and resist, as well as he can, the blandishment of his sorrow,
gives voice to his deep gloom. He consults with Phoebus' seer
and, drawing Mopsus aside, asks him what obtains:
"What can this plague mean, this mass depression we suffer?   400
Does it come from the mind of the gods? Is our weakness fate's decree?
Or do we, in our own hearts, exacerbate our troubles?
How long can we sit here forgetting our common purpose and hope
of home? How long can this anguish continue? And how will it end?"

    "I will give you my interpretation," said Mopsus,
"and explain the cause of this illness." He looked up at the stars

and after a moment continued: "We humans once were fire,
the kin of the gods, but now, in mortal frames, we suffer
and die after a span of life that at best is brief.

410 It is not right for men to kill one another, to hurry
with the reckless slaughter of sharp swords those souls that would tarry
a while longer on earth. The seed of the spirit returns
at last to heaven: we do not resolve into mere dust
the breezes can blow away; something remains, and anger
and grief, therefore, endure, and the dead, approaching the awesome
throne of Jove, cry out and complain of their piteous ends.
Sometimes the gate of death is opened again for them
so that they can return with one of the grim Sisters as guide
and together roam the earth and the seas, exacting vengeance

420 from all the guilt-stained souls of those who had been their foes,
tormenting them with the many and various terrors they've earned.
Those whose hands were dripping with innocent blood they have shed,
even by some mischance and with no intention of harm,
will contrive thus in their own minds to punish themselves
as their deeds come back to haunt them. Listless they are, and depressed
and despondent. They mope and weep, and their invalid spirits repine.
This is what you are seeing, but there may yet be a cure.
Part of the job of seer is remembering arcane things
that may someday prove useful. There is a far-off country

430 where Cimmerians live in a gloomy and desolate region. Their land
slopes away to the eerie silence of Stygian night.
Here the gods of Olympus never come: the Sun's
fiery chariot never approaches this place, and Jove's
star-appointed seasons make no stately procession.
Motionless, noiseless, the branches of trees seem to be painted
in thick clumps on the mountain ridges against a dreary
backdrop of leaden sky. Below them, a cavern gapes
and into its black maw a parade of spirits winds
its dolorous way. Nearby, the waves of Ocean break

440 and then withdraw to produce a series of sorrowful sighs,
the only sounds that infringe at all on this dreadful hush.
Here Celaeneus sits wearing a black great-cloak
and in his hand is a sword. Innocent men he cleanses,
remitting their burden of sin and appeasing resentful shades

whose anger he can assuage. He taught me what can be done
and how one must perform the rites of purification,
as he opened for me the great gates that lead from the earth
to Erebus' world below. When dawn breaks in the east,
and touches the sea with crimson, summon all your shipmates
for the sacrifice and bring for the gods a pair of beasts.   450
It would be wrong for me to approach until I have first
prepared myself through a night of devout and lustral prayer.
Apollo's chariot soon will be on its way. This task
we must see to at once. Order the men to keep still,
that no sound may distract me from the rites I'm about to perform."
    Sleep at this hour lay heavy on earth, and visions and dreams
flitted hither and thither over the silent crew,
as Ampycus' son, Mopsus, turned his face to the grove
and kept his vigil until it came time to make his way
to the river to commence the mystic rite. At its mouth   460
where Aesepus pours its fresh water into the brine
of Ocean, he bathed his body and scrubbed it to make it worthy
to undertake those awesome duties he faced. He prepared
a wreath of olive leaves for his head and with his sword
drew in the sand the mystic patterns the business required
in which at certain points he constructed a series of altars
to various gods and spirits, many of names unknown.
With branches he'd cut from the nearby trees he devised a roof
to shield from the sight of the skies a part of that sacred ground.
He summoned then these powers from beneath the earth and the sea   470
to attend at this silent sanctum. Then, from far down the beach,
a flash of light announced the procession was underway
of the men from the *Argo* marching in sacramental robes
and leading the sheep with the gilded foreheads as he had instructed.
Wearing a long white robe as Apollo's priest, he waved
a beckoning branch of welcome. They herd the sheep, which he blesses
with a touch of the god's laurel on each of their nodding heads.
The men proceed to the stream, remove their shoes, and weave
laurel leaves in their hair, and then, as Mopsus requires,
they raise their hands to greet the rising sun of Apollo   480
and fall down prostrate upon the beach to invoke the divine
compassionate relenting they hope to deserve. The sheep,

every one of them black as sin itself, they slay.
A certain part of the chines they reserve, but the rest Idmon
bears aloft as he marches among them along those lines
Mopsus has made in the sand, and again, and yet again,
touching each time he passes the men's armor and garments
and at last flinging the pieces into the depths of the sea.
Mopsus now put the choice morsels that they had kept back
490   into the altar's flames to sizzle and be consumed.
Oaken logs they had stripped of their bark and hewn to resemble
Argonauts were set out on the beach and dressed in armor,
and to these the priest refers the Stygian spirits' vengeance,
reassigning to them the guilt of the shedding of blood
, that he prays may weigh instead upon their wooden hearts,
as with remorseful keening he chants to the souls of the dead:
"Leave us, you who were slain, and forgo your righteous anger.
Let there be peace between us. Content yourselves, if you can,
in your Stygian resting place, far from our course on the sea,
500   and far from the perilous battles in which we are soon to engage.
Do not haunt our cities back home in Greece or assemble
in baleful swarms at our crossroads to shriek and moan in complaint.
Do not send plagues on our cattle or crops, or punish our people
with mean yields on their farms, or visit upon our blameless
children the harm your anger for what we did may prompt."
When he is done he sets on the leafy altars the last
portions of meat and pours on the earth a libation of wine
for which there are snakes that appear with open mouths to drink
with quick darting tongues, on behalf of the men who had just died.
510   Ampycides then gives orders that the ship be readied. The men
take their seats on the thwarts and row, and do not look back.
Let them forget the bloody deeds of their hands and of fate.
Quickly they stow their armor and weapons, while others set out
the cushions on rowers' benches. They fit their oars to the rowlocks
and manfully shout the stroke for the blades to bite in the water.
Think how, when Jupiter scatters a cloud that has stained the sky
and darkened the flanks of the mountains, the sun breaks through in glory
and the forests shine, and the peaks gleam in the sudden brightness
of a sky that has been transformed: so is the mood of the men
520   changed as the heroes' spirits revive. The helmsman calls

for a power twenty, and Eurytus, at Talaus' taunting, strips
and without his clothing's encumbrance vies with Idas, across.
And the others compete as well, their chests wet with their sweat
and the spume of the sea as they toil with great groans at their oars,
churning the sea with the steady pull, and again pull,
as they take delight in watching their widening wake recede.
Hercules joins in the sport and challenges all his shipmates,
"Who dares compete with me? Who else can row as hard?"
and he pulls on the shaft of his oar so hard that the good wood shatters,
and he falls back into Talaus' lap and knocks him down   530
and Eribotes beside him, and Amphion sitting across
has to lean away to avoid the great bulk of the hero
and bends down with his head almost in Iphitus' lap.

    Phoebus by this time has risen high up in the sky
beyond the midpoint where long shadows of men are shortened,
and the *Argo* makes its way somewhat more slowly now
without Hercules' strength as one of the rowers. Tiphys
steers for the nearest shore, a Mysian mountainside
thickly wooded, and lands to enable the hero from Tiryns
to venture into the ash grove and find some suitable tree   540
to fell for another oar, and Hylas, the youth, goes along
almost running to try to keep up with the hero's pace.

    From up in heaven's loftiest bastions, Juno looks down
and sees that he's left the ship, which gives her the chance she wants
to work on him that mischief she harbors within her bosom.
But first what she has to do is distract the vigilant Pallas,
who is guiding Hercules' steps so as not to delay the ship.
How can this be accomplished? She addresses her sister goddess:
"A war is brewing. Perses is driven out of his home
by his kinsman's army and now recruits barbarian troops   550
under Hyrcania's banners: Aeëtes, the king of Colchis,
is one, and his daughter's betrothed, the Albanian Styrus, arrives
to add his men to their force. A dreadful battle impends
that Mars will delight to behold, and he urges his baleful chargers
with a sharp flick of their reins. Look, you, to the North where a cloud
hangs in the gloomy sky. Hurry there to deliver,
when Perses crosses the Phasis and arrays his troops at the city's
walls, the news of the *Argo*'s approach. Contrive delays,

and let them discuss and parley. Promise him princes will come
560   who can claim their descent from the gods to join in Perses' fight."
The virgin goddess suspects that her stepmother's commission
may have an ulterior motive that her bland expression hides,
but what can she do? She complies, departing at once on her errand.
    Now left alone, Juno groans in her frustrated anger
and complains aloud: "This man seems immune to my hatred!
What more can I do? What other Nemean beast can I
contrive for him? What other monsters can I discover
like Lerna's horrible Hydra? I seem unable to daunt him,
and he volunteers for more, at Troy and at Pergamon's gates.
570   The sister of kings am I and I ought to have honor and power,
but by this man I am shamed, since that time when I sent the serpents
to kill him, a babe in his cradle, but they were the ones he killed.
I ought perhaps to have read that event as a sign and quit.
But, no, I press on with my purpose. Modesty I have put by,
and honor too, in this cause . . . The Furies and Dis himself
I shall recruit and, one way or another, I will defeat him."
Thus she speaks, and she looks to the pine-clad hills for prompting,
a thought of how to proceed, and coming across her field
of vision there is a band of lovely huntress nymphs,
580   the pride of the woods and the waters, wielding small bows and spears
fashioned of myrtle wood. Their skirts are short and their hair,
worn loosely, undulates as they run and sweeps their blouses
in which one can see the shapes of their saucy jouncing breasts,
while under their delicate footsteps the grass yields and recovers
like bedding. Dryope, one of their number, hearing the noises
of Hercules' advance and the flight of the game before him,
had stolen forward to see what was making this noise and beheld
the great man. She is now returning, her face awe-stricken.
This is the one whom Juno, descending to earth and leaning
590   against a convenient pine trunk, beckons and, grasping her hand,
addresses with coaxing words: "That suitor whom I have chosen
in preference to so many others, the one for whom you're intended,
is here, Hylas, arrived at last in the ship of the Greeks.
At this moment he wanders among your glades and hillsides.
You remember when Bacchus, the god, was led as his triumph's captive
by the hordes of an eastern kingdom and he stirred his followers' passions

for the sacred revels. Or think of Apollo, his lyre laid by,
and dressed in his sporting clothes for the hunt. Such a prize is Hylas!
How must the nymphs of Achaea bewail their loss, or the sprites
of Boebe's lake be sad at what has been taken away   600
from their domain. The yellow Lycormas' river nymphs
must also feel aggrieved and envy you your luck."
Saying which, she dispatches a swift stag through the brush
with a great rack on his head, and it crosses the young man's path,
and stops for a moment to graze. How can he not respond?
He follows the stag, of course, which bounds away, and he chases,
his huntsman's passion ablaze for so splendid and close a quarry,
and Hercules who sees this calls out encouraging words
as the lad disappears from sight. Hylas runs after the deer
as it cuts this way and that through the thick bushes and trees   610
and now and again he thinks he may have a shot, but the deer
darts away, and he follows wherever the animal goes.
They reach a spring that gushes, producing a sizable pool
over which the deer leaps in a graceful bound that the youth
cannot possibly match. Weary, baffled, he drops
to the ground to rest at the water's edge. He gleams with the sweat
that bathes his limbs, and his chest heaves from exertion. A trick
of the light, perhaps? The water's silvery surface shines
as it does when moonlight strikes it at night, or at midday, the sun
comes dappling down through leaves to gleam on the mirrored shimmer,   620
but he does not see in this brightness the nymph's shadow that passes
or notice her shining hair, or hear the watery plash
as Dryope now emerges to grasp him in sudden embrace.
He calls out in panic for help, for Hercules to come,
but the nymph is dragging him down and is helped by his falling weight.
     By this time the hero of Tiryns has found his ash tree and felled it
and wrapped its trunk in the hide of his lion skin to tote it
back to the shore. He assumes that Hylas has slain that stag
and found some other path to carry its carcass back
to their shipmates' banquet, but no, none of the men has seen him.   630
Where can he be? His friend and companion is . . . still in the woods?
Hercules' heart is heavy with all manner of fears
affection incites. Has he lost his way? Is he hurt? It is dark,
which is worrisome all the more. Panic grips him. His face

is chalky pale and the sweat pours down from his noble brow.
As sailors fear the winter storms that Jove can send,
or drovers worry when wolves howl in the gathering darkness,
so is Alcaeus' heir tormented by Hylas' absence,
and he thinks of implacable Juno, whose enmity knows no bounds.
640 Has she done something to hurt this boy? Like a tormented bull
a gadfly has bitten and crazed that breaks from Calabrian thickets
to charge and that nothing can stop or turn away, he rages,
and the whole forest quakes in its guilt, and the mountains tremble
at what the hero may now, in his grief's extremity, do.
They say that a lion when hit by a Moor's lance will go mad
and in agony run and roar and snap with furious jaws
that want to inflict hurt on its foe but close upon nothing,
nothing . . . So did the man of Tiryns go forth with his bow
strung and ready to shoot as he ranged over the hillsides.
650 Woe to any poor beast that should cross his path, and woe
to any innocent person he might, in his frenzy, encounter!
With no particular plan, he wanders the woodlands looking
this way and that, or follows the banks of the streams, or cuts back
into the shadows of trees he thinks he may recognize, calling
"Hylas!" again and again, "Hylas!" An answer? An echo
that mocks him and then dies away to an utter silence.

　　　Back at the ship, the crew is confident still, and the winds
are blowing fair, and they know they can leave without waiting for Hylas,
a pleasant enough youth, but expendable surely. His shipmate
660 Hercules is a man they will miss. It's for him they are waiting,
and some of them venture inland to look for him, calling his name,
which echoes along the shore, or waving their signal torches.
Their captain looks at the mountain, forbidding in darkness and silence,
and back at the sea the offshore breeze has smoothed, and he weeps
at the loss of this hero he loves and for whom he will linger longer,
though knowing now that it's useless. That lumbering gait, and the quiver
bouncing on that broad back, he's unlikely to see again.
He mourns for the hero's presence at the banquet table, the wine cup
grasped in his burly fist, while he tells his friends some story
670 of how he defeated one of those monsters his stepmother sent.

　　　Juno, relentless, bestirs the breezes the captain knows
are just what he needs, and Tiphys says aloud what he's thinking —

that any further delay is unrealistic and pointless.
Jason at last gives way, assembles the crew, and speaks:
"I wish I could say that the words the seer of Parnassus delivered
back when we were devising the Scythians' deaths were false.
I doubted the oracle then—that the strongest of all our crew,
the mightiest man of arms, would be taken from us by fate
and Jove's command and would never reach the wandering rocks
in that sea to which we are headed. And I still entertain some hope   680
that word of our companion may reach us at any moment.
But let us consult together and say what our hearts may prompt
as we consider the question the stirring breezes pose:
to set sail and continue the journey we've undertaken,
or not? Do we risk the further delay of another search?"
That was the choice he gave them, and the heroes seemed of one mind,
that they ought to put forth at once, for they were a group, a team,
and weren't their hands as strong as Hercules' or their hearts
every bit as noble? Such pride they had and such valiant
spirits. This kind of talk emboldened the undecided,   690
who had not spoken. So, in the forests, the beasts behave:
the proud stag will lead the herd; and the boar comes out
for battle; the she-bear is brave; and the howling wolves are defiant
and proud when the fierce tiger is gone and the lion they fear
is asleep in his cave somewhere. But Telamon, angry, speaks up
and the waves of his rhetoric's tide foam in his righteous anger
as he chides them all and defies their shameless lapse from the truth
and calls on the gods as his witness. Along with the others, Jason
listens, with downcast eyes, to the truth of these scathing words:
"What is this talk of teamwork? One of our team has gone missing!   700
Do we just sail away and leave him behind? Never mind
that it's Hercules! We are all comrades, and each of us counts,
and every man of the crew deserves better than this!
There's a wilderness we're facing with hostile savage tribes,
and it's madness to say that we have no need of Hercules' help.
Who else is as strong, whose heart is as mighty and noble as his?"
In answer to this, Meleagar, the Caledonian, answered
with clever but specious words that made the worse cause seem
the better but paid no mind to the ethical obligations
all of them ought to have felt or the deference due their leader.   710

"It is not my respect for the missing Hercules," he said,
"but only my duty to you that has kept me from speaking my mind
until invited to do so. But now that the subject is raised,
I say we have waited a week with South Wind blowing behind us
and could by now have beached our ship on those Scythian shores
for which we're bound. But we wait and waste our time, as if
we had forgotten the joys of returning home to our loved ones.
We are not exiles from cruel tyrants we've left behind.
I could better have spent these seven days we have lost
720   in Calydon's peace and plenty at the hearth of my parents' house.
What are we doing here? Why do we strain our eyes
staring at an expanse of the sea we ought to have crossed
already? Which of us thinks our shipmate may yet turn up
to join his quiver's arrows with yours and mine in battle
in the land of Phasis? Hatred is patient, and Juno does not
forget herself or her godhead or forgive the man she despises.
She has sent, I do not doubt, another monster or wraith
to trouble her stepson again, or perhaps this time destroy him.
We are missing a son of Jove, but Castor and Pollux can boast
730   of the same divine sire, and they are still here beside us.
I, who can also claim distinguished forebears, offer
my solemn pledge to follow and serve you just as well
in whatever fight we may face against any manner of foe.
Whatever may be required, even of my life's blood,
is yours to command. Indeed, I volunteer for the hardest
and most dangerous duty. For safety, we looked to him,
to Hercules, but I say that mortals are never secure.
We depend each on the others, as when we row, our oars
must move in coordination in equal strength and pace.
740   And as for him? Some madness may have overwhelmed his mind,
some aftereffect, perhaps, of the glory he has won
so that he holds in disesteem such communal efforts
as this upon which we're engaged, and for some such flimsy reason
refuses to share his fame with the likes of the rest of us.
I say to you all, be brave and with high hopes let us go forward
while our vigor is fresh and our limbs are strong. Is it not enough
to destroy the Colchian rabble? That was our common purpose
and why we invested our strength in crossing the perilous sea.

I'd hoped that he might return, and my friendship drove me, too,
to hunt for him through the forest, calling his name. Even now   750
I glance from time to time to the woods and expect to see him
descending the mountain's slope. But we've paid sufficient tribute
to sentiment and friendship and shed our abundance of tears.
Face the truth and assume that the hazards of hunting or fighting
have taken him out of our midst. Admit it, grieve, and go on."

    In these words did Oeneus' son Meleager stir up
the band of heroes. Calais endorsed what his shipmate had said
and urged that the hawsers be loosed at once. But Telamon differed,
could not understand the decision they seemed to have taken so lightly,
and felt in his heart deep sorrow. Should he quit his ship and companions,   760
dissociate himself from their callow action, and stay
to search the mountain heights for his lost friend? He complains:
"What a day is this for the Greeks! In Colchis, what joy will they feel
to see us behave in a manner that they would themselves disdain,
savages though they be? Remember when we embarked,
we all rejoiced and were grateful that Hercules would join us!
There were no ridiculous boasts back then that any of us
were his equals in strength or valor or birth. Has anything changed
from then to now? Is loyalty dead in us all, and honor?
There are tears that ought to be shed for the loss of Hercules!   770
Does Meleager propose himself as our leader now,
or Calais? Does the savage lamb attack the frightened
lion these days? I swear by the spear in my hand, the work
of the great Didymaon, a solemn oath and promise you all —
and what I say is as true as that this dead wood in the shaft
will never again sprout leaves as its mother tree once did
before it was put to use as a weapon — that one day, you,
our captain, will be in danger, and you will call out in vain
for the aid of Hercules, stronger and braver than anyone here,
that man whose arms you despised and abandoned, and all your boasting   780
and bragging you will on that terrible day have cause to regret."

    Meanwhile, Phorcys, the sea god, sends out a signal to summon
the barnacle-encrusted seals and sea lions who come
to gather at his cave mouth, while herdsmen, ashore, from distant
Crete to Marseilles or back in Calabria trudge from the fields
back to their homes as, far to the west, in the sky the sun

has yielded to night, and the delicate stars are out, and the breezes
have faded away as if at rest, and the sea is silent.
Amphitryon's son and heir has no idea where else
790 to search for his page, or which way to turn his steps, or what word
he can take home now of Hylas' fate to tell his father.
Should he rejoin his shipmates? Love for this youngster has seared
his heart and he cannot think of leaving these gloomy woods.
He is a lioness groaning in anguish for her lost cub,
prowling the paths, the roads, the fences of farms, and the walls
of towns in her anxious vigil. With her grief-stricken eyes she peers
in vain, and her unkempt mane sweeps the ground in despair.

Book IV

The Father of Gods could no longer bear to look down on his son—
so loyal and strong, and in anguish—with indifferent eyes but, moved
to pity, he turned to Juno, his anger's embers blazing
as he rebuked her, asking "Are you satisfied now? Are you happy?
The hero of Tiryns is going mad on that desolate shore,
and the Minyae, his faithless comrades, have sailed away and left him.
Is this how Juno takes care of her own? You're protecting Jason,
but sooner or later you're going to see him in trouble, afraid,
and beset by Scythian powers, and then you will come to me, begging
with a suppliant's tears and prayers for help for your favorite. Go,   10
stir up the Furies, arouse Venus, and ask them for help.
That wicked maiden of Colchis waits for the *Argo* to come,
and for her crimes I foresee that at last Aeëtes' sorrows
shall be avenged." He spoke and then he brought out the fragrant
mysterious nectar that has the soporific power
of deep and untroubled sleep. With it he touched the temples
of his suffering son, whose eyes grew heavy, although his lips
still cried aloud for Hylas. But mortals can never resist
the power of gods, and he sank to the ground and slept, and the woods
were at peace again, and the streams purled and the breezes murmured.   20
    And then, in a dream, he saw the boy rise up from the water,
oddly turned out in the saffron weeds in which the implacable
nymph had decked him. Approaching the sleeping hero, he says,
"It is useless to mourn, dear friend. This glade was appointed for me;
my fate was waiting here. Blame Juno, or else the naughty
nymph who stole me away but has won me the power to romp

with the spirits of woodland brooks and hillsides, and even consort
with gods. She has given me love and a share in the spring's honor
over which she presides. I bid farewell to my bow and quiver
30   and the joys of the hunt. Our comrades have undone the mooring cables
and sailed away on the winds at the urging of Meleager's
evil tongue, and for this he shall one day be punished,
when his mother does to him what you might have wished yourself.
Awake, arise, and be brave in adversity's face, assured
that you shall one day ascend to the heavens where stars shall bear you
high in your well-earned glory. Until then, let my love
provide you with strength and comfort. O friend, remember me."
The sleeper groans and his arms reach out in vain to embrace
the ghostly presence. He rouses himself, but the boy is gone,
40   and his tears well up afresh. He would follow, give chase . . . But where?
They say that, at sea, when those halcyon birds build floating nests,
the waves sometimes overturn them or carry them onto a rock
and the mother bird in her horror hovers over the water,
crying and darting down in attempts to follow her chicks
as her flimsy home is broken and sinks, and she soars and screams
in inconsolable anguish. Such was the hero's dream.
He staggers, his cheeks are wet with his streaming tears, and he answers
the empty air of the woods: "How can I leave you here
alone on this barren hillside? Oh, my dear boy, my exploits
50   without your admiration mean nothing whatever to me."
He retraces his steps through the woods and back to the shore, unsure
what new disaster Juno may have readied for him in her spite.
He reaches the beach to watch the ship disappear in the offing,
and is shamed that his comrades without any word of fare-thee-well
have sailed away to leave him behind, alone and abandoned.

    He turns his steps to Troy and Laomedon's promised horses,
but just at this moment Latona comes before Jove with Diana,
her daughter, and son, Apollo, and they stand before his throne,
their eyes full of grief. Apollo, in supplication, speaks:
60   "How long can these torments last that Prometheus suffers each moment?
If Hercules does not come to his aid, how can he endure
the pains to which you've condemned him? The race of mankind begs
that justice be tempered with mercy. His theft of fire was wicked,
a betrayal of heaven's secrets, but for how long must he continue

writing there?" At this instant, on a distant crag in the mountains,
Prometheus groans as the ravening vulture tears at his vitals
and raises his eyes that the frost has all but closed to the skies,
as the rivers cry out and even the rocks in their sympathy hum.
The horrid bird is distracted. From Acheron's deeps, a cry
of Iapetus rises in pleading, but the Erinys thrust him aside   70
and look to Jove and insist on his law's letter. But he
is moved by the goddesses' tears and Apollo's stately persuasion
and dispatches Iris to go on her rosy cloud to convey
his message to Hercules: "Let him postpone his business
with Troy and send him to rescue the Titan from that vile bird."
At once, the goddess departs and flies to the hero to speak
into his eager ear and convey to him the command
that he perform the task his father Jove has set him.

    The Minyae, meanwhile, have sailed through the clear and starry night
and their bellying sails have carried them out of sight of the shore.   80
There in the darkness beneath the whirl of the constellations
their minds spun with remorse for the man they had left behind,
but then, from the poop, the bard of Thrace took up his lyre
that soothes the troubled souls of men, and Orpheus sang
his sweet songs to his comrades to relieve their pain and heal
their spirits' griefs so that joy could return to their hearts, as parents
know how to jolly their children, whose wailings abruptly pass.

    The stars were gliding westward and into the Ocean's source,
and the jingle of horses' bridles were sounding in caves in the east
where Phoebus stables his steeds. At the Hours' prompting, the Sun   90
put on his splendid tiara of dazzling rays and his sash
woven of starlight and fastened with the rainbow belt we see
sometimes festooning the sky as it cuts across somber clouds.
Above the earth and over the peaks of the eastern mountains
his brilliance arose in the sky to bedazzle the sparkling waves
over which the Minyae were rowing as the breezes died away.

    They approached the Bebrycian shore. In this land of fertile soil,
famous for nurturing bulls of distinctive size and strength,
King Amycus ruled, who trusted the gods' powers and fate,
for his subjects built no walls and made no laws for themselves   100
or treaties with other nations, but lived in a savage state
entirely unconstrained. As the Cyclopes who dwell

in their caves on Aetna's slopes peer out at the straits during storms
in the hope that the fierce South Wind may drive some ships aground,
providing Polyphemus with his shore dinner of wretched
sailors' body parts, so these preposterous Asians
look out at the water, hoping for crews they can take as captives
back to their king, whose custom is flinging them over a cliff
in sacrifice to his father, Neptune, the great sea god —
110 but he makes exceptions of men with athletic prowess. These
he offers the chance to live and to box with the deadly cestus
with his talented native goons, who kill them just as surely,
but it's slower this way and more painful, and makes a much better show.
In the depths of the sea Neptune watched as the vessel approached
his son's domain and he sighed, and addressing the ash nymph who bore him,
Melia, he said, "A pity that I once carried you off
and not my Thunderer brother. The fate that awaits our son
is woeful indeed. I cannot remember when Jove was so cruel,
except to unlucky Orion, whom Diana's arrow dispatched.
120 The powers that influence gods are complicated, and Jove
has other considerations than those of our ties of blood.
For this reason I could not turn the winds and the tides
against the course of this ship that comes with its cargo of death
for the son of our union, but still I grieve and wish there were other,
lesser kings that implacable hero was bound to destroy."
He turned away, a father leaving his child to suffer
in a cruel and bloody fight he was destined, this time, to lose.

        The captain, reaching the shore, dispatches a squad to explore
along the beach and the banks of the river where they have moored
130 and discover what manner of people they are who dwell in these parts.
Echion leads the way and the first man he encounters
is a sorrowing youth who sits on the ground in a sheltered hollow
and laments that his friend is murdered, but he looks up and is startled
by the stranger's sudden and odd appearance — he wears a hat
in the broad-brimmed Arcadian style that Mercury, his father,
often affects, but he carries the olive branch of peace.
The youth, whose name, it turns out, is Dymas, warns him to flee.
"Whoever you are, get out. Get away while you still can."
Echion hears these repeated warnings and tries to get more
140 in the way of detail. At length, when he brings the young man with him

to tell the rest of the crew his story, Dymas explains
with a broad sweep of his arm: "It's a dreadful place you've come to,
where the rites of guest and host are altogether ignored.
This is the coastline of death and cruel battles they call
sport. Their king is Amycus, and he promotes the bouts,
challenging you to put on the cestus—the killing glove—
and fight to the death for glory. He claims to be Neptune's son
and he hates sailors, insults them, and says that they all are cowards,
are afraid of his fighters, and only good as a sacrifice
to be led to an altar for slaughter like so many stupid cattle.   150
He taunts you until you fight, which is what he wants—to watch
wretches' brains get spattered. Listen to me. Take off
while you still have the chance. This king is a monster it's useless to challenge.
There's nothing here worth fighting *for*." The chief of the *Argo*
replies with a question: "Are you a Bebrycian who tells us this,
a renegade or a traitor estranged from your ruler here?
Or are you a stranger whom fate has brought to these shores? And how is it
that you have been spared by Amycus' dreadful cestus?" The other
answers, "I came with my dear companion, Otreus, brother
of Lycus of whom you have heard, the king of the Mariandyni.   160
He came in quest of a Phrygian bride—for Hesione's hand—
and Amycus offered the challenge to fight. I laced up the gloves.
And the moment my friend stepped into the ring, Amycus hit him,
a shattering blow that knocked his eyes from his broken head.
Me, he dismissed as not worthy of a hero's death, and left me
here to weep these bitter tears and consume myself
in hopeless, helpless grief. What can I do? Send home
a message to Lycus to come to try to avenge his brother's
death and his people's dishonor? Better, by far, he remain
at home. What earthly good will it do for another man   170
to put on those gloves to fight and suffer the same hard end?"

    The young men of the *Argo*'s crew listen, impassive,
to this report, or complaint, but do not react. He beckons
that they should follow and see for themselves this madman's work.
They hurry along the beach to a large cave at the base
of a steep cliff in the shadow of trees that grow at the top.
No light of the sun can reach this barren place, a grim
and eerie spot that echoes with endless sounds of the waves

that break on the rocks, among which they make out pieces of bodies,
180   human arms unconnected to any torsos but wearing
Amycus' cruel cestus. Among these are various bones,
some picked clean and others with tatters of rotting flesh.
And skulls, a pile of them, some of them grinning grotesquely and some
so badly shattered as hardly to seem to have once borne names
and faces. Among these pathetic pieces of Amycus' victims
were strewn the weapons he and his people had used to kill them,
now offered up on this woeful altar he'd made for his father
or else abandoned—but who would touch them, knowing to whom
they once had belonged? What Dymas had told them now seemed convincing,
190   and they felt the icy grip of fear at their hearts as they looked
at one another's faces, astonished, disgusted, appalled.
Pollux, at length, spoke up: "Whoever you are who did this
terrible deed, if you have limbs, then you, too, can be
dismembered, and if there is blood in your veins, then you, too, can bleed.
I will add your body to the meat-case display of this beach."
The others, hearing his words, took courage and volunteered
that they were also ready to try their strength and meet
this monstrous person in combat, and they called out into the air
their challenge and their defiance. So, when cattle have come
200   to a river that foams in flood, there is always one brave bull
that tries the water's dangerous eddies to show the way
is not yet blocked and then the others wade in to follow
or even in midstream will forge ahead to lead.

        From the woods on the cliffs above, the ruthless and powerful king
is herding his sheep and descending to the cave's mouth. His people
are in awe of him, and with reason, as mountain men will avoid
a lofty and dangerous peak cut off from the rest of the range.
He hurries down the beach, his anger aroused by these men,
whoever they are, and their presence as much as their shouted challenge.
210   He does not ask who they are or where they have come from, but thunders
in bitter wrath: "You are fools or madmen! What lured you here?
No doubt it was stories you've heard of the welcome we offer to tourists?
Or have you been blown off course and ventured ashore not knowing
what land this is? I will tell you: it's Neptune's kingdom, and I
am Neptune's son, and the law and custom that I have established
is to fight with any strangers whom folly or boldness brings here.

Before they reach the seas and enormous steppes of Asia,
they have to pass this coastline, and the gauntlet I throw down,
or cestus, rather. The contest is one that only a king
so far has survived and lived. I mean, of course, myself.   220
A long time has passed since I last refreshed this display
with new blood, bones, and teeth. Who will volunteer?
Who accepts my challenge? Who will strive for the prize
we all in the long run win—a hall pass into Hades?
There is no escape, no way through the air or under the earth.
And my heart is as hard as these rocks. It's no good trying to beg
or appeal to my better nature (I haven't got one) or heaven.
My father, remember, is Neptune, and Jupiter rules elsewhere.
I have my father's warrant to keep Bebrycian waters
free of unwanted intrusion, so the clashing rocks beyond   230
that every vessel dreads still close their jaws upon nothing."
     In answer to these offensive and provocative words, Jason
strode forward, and just behind him both of Aeacus' sons,
Telamon and his brother Peleus, and with them
the Caledonians, Meleager and Tydeus, clenching
their fists, and Neleus' son, Periclymenus, and Idas,
each and every one of them puissant heroes, but Pollux
had made his way to the fore, and had already bared his breast
in preparation for fighting. His brother Castor looked on
in apprehension, wondering whether this piece of work   240
was more than Pollux could handle. This was no sporting match
of gentlemen back in Sparta with a referee and rules,
where the victor could bathe himself in his pleasant native streams
and delight in his prize—a bull or a stallion with pounding hooves.
Here the winner's only trophy would be the corpse
of the fighter he had defeated. Amycus smiled, or sneered,
as he looked at this youngster before him, not huge in build or fierce
in bearing and visage. His face, instead of whiskers, had down
that had just begun to darken. Amycus rolled his bloodshot
eyes in a show of annoyance or maybe contempt. He was like   250
Typhoeus, boasting the battle with heaven's kingdom was won
even before it began, looking across at Bacchus
and Pallas—a mere boy and a girl with snakes on her hat.
Amycus all but laughed as he told his opponent, "Come on,

whoever you are. I'm ready. I'll smash that pretty face.
What's left of you not even your mother will recognize!
A hell of a set of friends you have, who will let you die
here, now, by my hand . . ." And then there were no more words
but a demonstration as Amycus strutted and postured, flexing
260   his arms' and his torso's muscles. The Minyae's spirits quailed
as they saw what Pollux was facing, and he was himself abashed.
They remembered now those foolish things they had said of their shipmate
Hercules, whose help they'd be grateful for right now,
and some even looked around to the hills and the empty sea.
Neptune's son then produced the hardened bull's-hide gloves.
"Put these on," he said, "and then let the best man win,"
and he spat, snorted, and added, "whatever sense that makes."

He had no idea that this would be the comeuppance that fate
had prepared for him, but he turned to his seconds, who got him ready,
270   put on his gloves and laced them, as Pollux was likewise prepared.
They glared at each other, strangers but enemies now, and hatred
welled up in the beating hearts of Jove's and Neptune's sons
as they entered the circle. Around them, the men were hushed in suspense
as their minds wavered from hope to fear and back again,
and they thought of the many ghosts who had been this monster's victims,
to whom they prayed to appear — and a cloud darkened the sky
of these shades Hades had sent at the least to bear mute witness
and perhaps to see that moment of retribution these souls
of the slain had thirsted for. The Bebrycian chieftain comes on
280   like a storm that sweeps from Malea's height down to the sea,
and Pollux can scarcely withstand the assault or hold up his head
or keep up his guard. A rain, a torrent of Amycus' blows,
and a bearing down of that bulk of muscle and bone that pursues,
but Pollux dodges and feints and shifts this way and that,
bobbing his head and dancing forward and back on tiptoe
with steps that are hard to predict. He darts in, jabs, and retreats,
and the force of Amycus' onslaught is like some squall at sea
when a ship that a skillful helmsman negotiates through the waves,
bobbing, pitching, and yawing, somehow stays on course.
290   Pollux is like that vessel, avoiding the force of the punches
so that Amycus' fists keep missing and he wears himself out as he throws
blow after savage blow into what turns out to be air.

Then, when Amycus' arms are slower, heavier, tired,
and Pollux can hear his stertorous breathing and see his sweat,
he comes in with more than a feint or a single jab but attacks
with combinations to head and body that land and hurt.
None of his people has seen this happen to Amycus, ever.
He's tired, hurt, and confused as he backs off to rest for a moment,
much in the way the Lapiths paused in their brawl to wait
for Mars to refresh their spirits. They stand for a moment glaring   300
and then they are at it again with another flurry of blows,
uppercuts, left hooks, right crosses, the sound of the gloves' landing
painful even to hear. One is ashamed, while the other,
Pollux, now feels some hope that fuels his body's engine.
Having lasted this long, he figures he can perhaps continue
to wear his opponent down, tire him out, keep on
hitting the body with punches that make the man's sweat splash.
The pounding is like an anvil's, when the Cyclops prepares the bolts
Jove will throw and the clang of his labors resounds in the night.
Pollux moves in and feints with his right to make Amycus lunge,   310
but then with a hard left he takes the man off balance,
smashes his face, and rocks him back, and his friends cry out
in sudden joy. The Greek draws back from the other's fury,
but Amycus, moving forward, has lost his concentration.
Going on instinct, he flails in helpless rage, throws punches
that miss, and again the exulting Minyae cheer their shipmate.
Amycus still comes on, throwing lefts and rights that Pollux
dances away from. He strikes again for the head and misses
but lands a blow to the chest, and another, and Amycus' punches
are missing now, but even the ones that land are weaker.   320
Pollux turns to the side to dodge a desperate attempt
that leaves Amycus open, and Pollux plants his legs
and peppers the side of his head with punch after punch, each shot
snapping the head back. Amycus staggers, helpless now,
at Pollux's mercy, and taking a terrible beating. His knees
are giving way and he sinks beneath the rain of leather
with blood coming out of his ears and down his temples, and Pollux
gives him a last terrible blow that snaps the bones
in the neck, and then he goes down like a stone, as dead as a stone.
Standing above him the victor cries in triumph: "I am   330

Pollux, the son of Jove. From Amyclae I come.
Announce to the wandering shades who it was who sent you there,
and know that my name shall be inscribed upon your tomb."

At this point the poor Bebrycians scatter like so many birds
in flight to the woods and the mountains, freed of the tyrant's oppression
under which they have languished. That ogre on guard at the wild Pontus
lies on the ground like the scree of an avalanche from a mountain,
from Athos perhaps, and Pollux inspects the corpse close up
as if to persuade himself that the monster is truly dead.

340　His shipmates and friends are rejoicing and crowd around to cheer
and lift him up on their shoulders and hold up his gloves, shouting:
"Way to go, Pollux! Hurrah for the son of Jove! Well done!"
There is also praise for the gyms back home where Pollux learned
to fight and his old coaches and trainers and sparring partners
who deserve to share in this triumph. Pollux, meanwhile, is smiling
and he dabs with his fists at the blood that still flows from a wound
on the side of his forehead where Castor is decking his brow with the laurel
of victory's wreath that he prays his brother may wear one day
when they all return to Greece, successful, famous, alive.

350　To propitiate the god who was Amycus' father, they offer
in sacrifice to Neptune fine steers from their herd
and for purification they bathe themselves in his sacred sea.
Then they lie on the ground on couches of leaves for their feast
and of course Pollux is given the choicest portions of meat
in sign of his comrades' approval, to which he responds with thanks
and joy, and he basks in their praise and the bard's song of his deed,
and twice he pours out libations of wine to honor his father.

The breeze is blowing and therefore they take to the sea again
and approach the Bosporus' narrows where the gelid water flows.

360　This is the "Cow's passage," which takes its name from Io,
who, before she became a goddess, crossed here on her way
to the Nile. Then Orpheus, bard, the son of Oeagrus, took up
his lyre, invoked his mother Calliope's aid, and sang
the story of Io, Inachus' daughter, changed to a heifer
who roamed the seas in exile, and his eager shipmates listened:
"In our fathers' time, it was often that Jupiter used to descend
to earth to the land of the Argives looking for pretty young girls.
Juno, not unaware of what these excursions were for,

also came down to earth, hot on his trail and with righteous
anger that burned in her heart. The Peloponnese was afraid   370
and every pleasant bower that Jupiter might have used
trembled in fear at the vengeance the Queen of Heaven might wreak.
To protect his paramour and deceive his wife, Jove turned
Io into a heifer, but Juno was not so stupid.
Why would her lord and master suddenly choose as a hobby
cattle ranching? And why would he have so small a herd?
She approached the beast, caressed it, managed a smile of approval
as she praised the creature's expression and carriage, and asked her husband
to give it to her as a pet. 'I can find it a pretty pasture,
one with a spring she can drink from. Look how her little horns   380
are just coming in! What a dear, sweet thing she is!' How could he
refuse his wife's request? What excuse could he make? What trick
could he, on the instant, devise? He manufactures a smile
and gives her the heifer. She takes it and sets Argus to guard it,
he with the hundred sleepless eyes like the peacocks' tails
that Lydian women work in needlepoint on their gowns.
Argus drives the heifer into rough country, on rocky
paths through the dangerous woods and mountainsides where monsters
of all manner are lurking. She's frightened and wants to complain
but cannot express what is in her heart, as the gift of language   390
is not given to heifers. As she crosses the furthest limits
of her father's lands she gives the ground a farewell kiss.
The fountain Amymone wails in farewell, and Messeis' waters
likewise wail, and Hyperia gurgles a plaintive good-bye,
while she, exhausted, her legs about to give way from fatigue,
is driven on through the darkness and cold that heaven pours
on her poor head. She lies down at last on the stony ground.
Her thirst compels her to drink from brackish pools. Her shoulders
are scored by the lash of her cruel drover. In utter despair
she looks for a cliff from which to leap to end her torment,   400
but Argus' kindness is cruel and he saves her as Juno would wish
for the further impositions his mistress has contemplated.
But then there is heard the soothing sound of a hollow flute
in the sweet Arcadian mode, as Mercury, heeding his father's
urgent bidding, comes to distract the hundred-eyed Argus.
'Listen,' he says. 'You deserve a rest. You can pause for a bit,

indulge yourself, and enjoy these elegant languorous tunes
I'm playing for you.' He performs and Argus' eyelids droop,
all of them, as he drifts away into gentle slumber,
410 whereupon the wingèd god whips out a gleaming
blade and lops off his head. Io resumes her human
shape and walks erect, thinking herself triumphant
over the Queen of Heaven. But then Tisiphone comes
with her burning brands and coiling serpents and fiendish cries
that terrify Io, who quickly resumes her heifer shape
and ambles away to arrive at length at Inachus' waters,
home—but how entirely changed she is! Her father
and all the nymphs, unable to recognize her, shun her.
Bereft, she returns to the pathless woods to flee from them all
420 as from the Styx itself and wander the world—through Greece,
its towns and its hills and rivers, until she is stopped by the sea,
where she hesitates but then in her recklessness plunges in.
Deferential, the waters part, as the ocean, aware
of what the future holds, obliges her by providing
a path for her dainty hoofs. Sunlight glints on her horns
and she holds her dewlaps high as she dances along, half walking
and half swimming across. Meanwhile, Tisiphone flies
through the air to Egypt, to Memphis, which she knows is where Io is headed.
But the Nile rises up to resist her and plunge to his sandy bed
430 the wicked spirit from hell. She calls on Dis for help,
and all the infernal powers. Along the shore are her whips
and other paraphernalia, the brands and the poison serpents
strewn from her punk coiffure. Meanwhile Jove in his anger
thunders from lofty heaven, and Juno trembles to hear him.
Io, watching this storm from Pharos' height, is transformed
and finds that she has become a goddess, the Isis Egyptians
worship: she holds in her hand a sistrum, a kind of wind chime,
and now it is *her* hair that's bedecked with coiling serpents.
·Thus have these waters in which we sail long borne her name—
440 Bos-porus, where the cow once made her miraculous passage.
Let us pray that she favor our labors and send fair winds
to help us now as we travel through the strait she knows as her own."

His tale was now concluded, and the wind, picking up behind them,
billowed the sail. The dawn was breaking to show their night's

progress: they now were abeam of the Thynian shores and the dreadful
torments Phineus suffered, the price the gods were exacting
for his canny mantic gift. In exile, and blind, he endured
the horrible Harpies' visits when they stole the food from his mouth.
Typhoeus' implacable daughters and the agents of Jove's wrath,
they waited upon him at table and in glee befouled his meals.   450
His only hope was that fate had decreed that he might be saved
by sons of North Wind, Boreas' boys, who now were Minyae
and on their way. He walked the shore, a broken man
and blind, groping along with his stick, until, at last,
the *Argo* appeared. "Hail," he says. "In you my prayers
are answered. I know who you are and the gods from whom you descend,
and I know your journey's purpose and what you have undergone
on your way here at Lemnos Island and Cyzicus' land
and on the Bebrycian beach, and have given my thanks for each day
that has brought you closer: you are my saviors and only hope.   460
This is not the moment for elaborate introductions
in which I could say how my father was the great Agenor, son
of Neptune and king of Phoenicia, or tell how Apollo gave me
my prophet's powers that led to my present woeful condition.
All you need know is what you see before you—a man
who has lost his sight and his homeland and wanders about in a dark
and hostile world. My complaints are boring, even to me.
When I sit down at table, the Harpies swoop overhead
like a black cloud that gathers. I can hear the flap of their wings
and I know Celaeno is coming to snatch food from my hand,   470
upset plates and cups, and befoul what I have not touched.
What random scraps that fall from their filthy claws, I eat
to cling to a life of which each passing moment I loathe.
But I believed in heaven's promise that you might save me
and have clung to this one hope I beg you not to dash.
You are those sons of North Wind who may rid me of these vile
birds, for I am a kinsman: my wife was Cleopatra,
the sister of Boreas' sons, Calais and Zetes, your shipmates."
　　These two at once come forward and Zetes asks of the man,
"Is it you? Phineus? Here? What has become of your glory?   480
You who were king of Thrace are devoured now by grief!
But do not despair, for now we have come, and whatever the gods'

wrath may allow we will surely do to improve your lot."
Phineus raised his hands to heaven and uttered this prayer:
"First, O Thunder god, I supplicate you and beg
that you show my gray hairs mercy. Let there be some limit
to the sentence you have imposed." Then to the youths he said,
"Heaven's goodwill I believe I have, for heaven has sent you.
That sin for which I am punished was nothing cruel or evil
490   but only an indiscretion — that I had revealed to men,
for the sake of the pity I felt for their human condition, heaven's
secret plans. For this, the darkness in which I live
was imposed on me, and the plague of Harpies that hover about me.
But the wrath of the gods is perhaps appeased, for you have arrived,
and no mere chance has brought you, but heaven's divine scheme
has led you here to this shore." Thus he spoke, and the men
were deeply stirred by the words of this bravely suffering man.
They set out their couches and cushions and invited him to recline
and join in their feast and, watching the skies offshore and inland,
500   they bade him put by his cares and eat. Then did he tremble
and his fingers carrying food to his agèd lips dropped down
as the birds in an instant appeared with an evil mephitic stench
that filled the air like a rank exhalation their sire's Avernus
might have emitted. They bother none, nor swarm to attack
any but Phineus, over whose head they hover to harry,
pouring forth on the cloth a stream of their gleaming shit
as Celaeno and her sisters turn the bountiful meal
to a nightmare of disgust and deprivation. The wingèd
sons of Boreas rise up with a shout to attack them, and, startled,
510   the monsters flee, dropping their stolen dainties and flying
inland to wheel for a moment over Phineus' palace roof
and then, in their fright as Calais and Zetes pursue them, retreating
out to sea, while the Greeks on shore gaze out at the sky
to watch as they dwindle away. It is said in Vesuvius' spasms
the thunder has scarcely subsided when a rain of ash comes down
to coat the towns on the coast. In such a malign whirlwind
do these birds pass over the peoples of islands and coastal towns
as they cross the sea, but Boreas' sons, relentless, do not
allow them to light or settle until they have reached the rocky
520   Strophades, the islands of turning, that is, where the winds

shift when sailors approach. There they swoop and hover,
weary, in mortal fear, and crying in dreadful shrieks
to their father, Typho, who comes to their aid, bringing his darkness
into the world of light. From the heart of the gloom a rich
sepulchral voice booms out to the wingèd youths: "Enough!
You have chased the goddesses here. Why pursue any farther
Jupiter's faithful agents? Let go your righteous rage
and be content to know that by their own master's order
they have no more to do with Agenor's son. To Jove
they defer, as you must do, yourselves. One day you shall know   530
their terror when the fated, fatal arrow is shot
that will bring you down. Meanwhile, the Harpies have other victims
to prey upon for their sustenance, for mortals are by their nature
weak and sinful creatures and arouse the anger of gods."
Calais and Zetes stopped in the air and fluttered in place.
Then, in assent and in triumph, they returned to their shipmates' ranks.
   The Minyae, meanwhile, renewed their sacrifice to Jove
to celebrate the release of Phineus from these monsters,
setting out once again the wine and the meat at the festive
couches, while in their midst Phineus sighed in relief   540
and delight as he enjoyed once again the bounties of Ceres
and the rare gifts of Bacchus as well as the simple forgotten
pleasure of cold, pure water to quench a parched man's thirst.
Jason was pleased to behold him enjoying in peace this plenty
in which, having survived his ordeal, he could partake.
Jason addressed him, asking, "Reverend sir, I implore you,
now that your prayers have been answered, give me the answers to mine.
Let me know what we face in these labors that we have begun.
Thus far we have come through and our luck has held good, but the risk
is great and the sea is wide on which we've embarked. Minerva   550
herself helped us prepare the vessel, and Juno gave aid
as we were recruiting our crew. But my mind is not yet easy.
The closer we get to Phasis, the more I find myself fretful
considering in my mind the enormous tasks before us.
What do we face? How well will we do? Though our seers have gifts,
what Mopsus and Idmon tell me leaves me with questions and doubts . . ."
Phineus let him go on no further but granted his wish
and, taking up the prophet's fillets and laurel wreath,

he summoned again those familiar mantic powers. Jason
560 watched in amazement the transformation, as though his burden,
those years of Jupiter's harsh sentence, were suddenly lifted,
and an old robustness braced his body and strengthened his limbs,
but yet he maintained the solemn dignity age deserves.
With authority nothing short of majestic he gave his answer
and riddled out the truth of the future's store of secrets:
"You, sir, who travel the lands of the earth in fame and glory,
you, whom the gods are helping and guiding, whom Pallas assists
and Pelias, all unknowing, propels to immortal fame
(for he never in all his wildest dreams expected to see
570 Jason bring back that golden fleece of Phrixus' ram),
you will hear from me what it is that your destiny holds
and the places you shall visit. The least I can do to show you
my gratitude is to let you know what trials await you
and how you will fare. The future's secrets are hidden from men,
but by Jove's particular warrant, my speech to you is inspired.
From here, your way lies north to the mouth of the Pontus in which
the Cyanean rocks await that wander across the water,
clashing in fury to crush their rocky cliffs together
and falling apart again. No ship have they ever seen,
580 for no one has dared defy their violent motion that shakes
the world's very foundation: the ground shudders, and houses
along the coast and even inland tremble and quake.
But heaven, perhaps, will help you, for you will require help
and wisdom, too, for your venture upon an uncharted sea
from which even the birds keep away and the winds avoid.
Neptune himself, uneasy about this part of his realm,
guides the reins of his frightened steeds in other directions.
What you must do is find a moment when these great rocks
delay, and take advantage of that unusual chance
590 to make your sudden dash. They separate and retreat
and they reach the opposing shores, but then with a roar of water
of enormous roiled waves they rush together again
like mountains charging each other, and blue-green brine sluices down
their oncoming flanks. But know in this crisis my prayers are with you,
for when Jove in his wrath dispatched those dreadful flapping birds
to plague my days, a voice from heaven announced: 'Know this,

O son of Agenor, your troubles will only end when a ship
has breached this forbidding sea and the clashing rocks have been stilled.
Until that comes to pass, you have no hope of pardon
or your punishment's end.' So spoke the god. Our fates are bound   600
together, for you must pass those rocks or the birds will be back,
unwanted guests at my table. But if you succeed, I am free.
Then you will come to the realm of Lycus, a civilized man,
a generous, welcoming host, returning home from his triumph
along the Bebrycian shores. But pestilence there awaits you,
and if any of your shipmates is stricken, do not lose heart
but remember that this was foretold, and bear it bravely. The future's
challenges still await you. But what good can I do you
by telling you now of the perils of Carambis' precipitous cliffs
over which the high clouds scud, or the whirling waters of Iris'   610
river, or Ancon's stream? Beyond those landmarks, you reach
the plain where the Thermodon flows. There the Amazons live,
who sprang from the great god Mars, the warrior women his sister
Enyo approves for their fierceness, for they can defeat most men,
and Pallas loves them also, who carries the Gorgon shield.
Do not let the mischievous winds drive your vessel ashore
anywhere near those dangerous regions where battle's clangor
constantly sounds in the air and hoofbeats shake the ground
as their father spurs them on with their brandished spears to combat.
For the Chalybes' race you need have no concern, for they   620
are crude but pacific, farming their grudging rocky fields
while at their hearths and anvils they forge their weapons and tools,
but pass them by all the same and set your course for the Phasis'
mouth, where a Scythian army has pitched its camp for battle.
There you shall throw your weight on the side of the forces of Colchis,
who one day shall be your foes. I see no further perils.
It may well be that your fate is to gain that fleece you seek
and bring it home, but do not put all your trust in strength
and courage. Remember that wisdom is often better than these,
and best of all is luck, or what heaven deigns to grant.   630
What awaits you then in the end, I am not allowed to reveal.
I pray you, let me be mute." And here he made an end
and, wrapping his head in his cloak, shrouded the rest in silence.
    An uneasy moment, and Jason, to prevent the spread of fear

in his comrades' hearts, gave orders that quickly they should prepare
the ship and resume their voyage. Phineus, there on the beach,
bade the brave men farewell, and he asked of Boreas' sons,
"What reward can I give you? How can I show my thanks?
My youth is restored, as if I were back in my native Tyre
640   on the heights of Mount Pangaeus, where the dawns break in their glory . . .
Are those vile birds really gone? Am I able again to dine
with nothing to fear? I offer my heartfelt gratitude
and send you all on your way with an old man's fervent abrazzo."
They pulled away from the shore and the land slipped out of sight.

　　　But then there comes to the men the dismal thought of those rocks
and the difficult problem they pose. From which side will they come?
Do they give some kind of warning? With faces set against fear,
the men peer out to port and starboard, but then they hear
the deep sound and, before they see the rocks themselves,
650   they notice the churning surface, the eddy and chop of the water
as if it were trying to flee their ship — or something larger
that harries it. Then they see them, the huge moving mountains
coming apart, and the sailors in shock let go their oars.
But Jason, climbing up on the thwarts of the ship, calls out
to encourage them or chide them: "Where are your loud boasts now?
We have been afraid before at the mouth of Amycus' cave
but nobody showed his terror. We held our ground and prayed
that the gods in heaven would show their favor to valor. The gods
are not fickle, do not change, and may come to our aid
660   once again if we do not allow our panic to show."
Having said this, he slips into Phalerus' place and seizes
the terrified rower's oar. The others, filled now with shame,
pull along to the stroke of their leader, but as they work
the boat is tossed around by a monstrous wave that the rocks
have thrown up as they crashed together and came apart
with a great noise and a shower of sparks from the smashing cliffs.
They have barely righted the boat and set it back on its course
when the rocks come together again with another wave and the spray
rises high in the air, where the sea and the sky are mingled
670   as they are sometimes in the worst typhoons when lightning rips
from the belly of black clouds to ignite the night and show
the stark terror on all the faces that ghastly glimpse

reveals to the men who huddle together from gasp to gasp
through the sheets of spray the ocean throws up as it writhes and rages.
    At this point, the gods looked down in concern to see how the vessel
might somehow contrive to pass where the rocks were blocking its way.
What can the crew devise to avoid the disastrous failure
into which they appear about to sink? The virgin
goddess is moved to help them and she hurls a bolt of lightning
that streaks down through the sky between the rocks, and the crew,   680
taking this for an omen, feel their courage return
and their strength, too, as Jason cries out to earth and sky,
"Whatever god you may be, I will trust in you and follow
wherever you lead, in the faith that this is no cruel deception."
The men row and the boat speeds headlong into the uproar,
that mixture of smoke and spume where the mountains are giving way,
and the ebbing waves pick up the keel and speed it across
to the open sea that lies beyond it. But now the rocks
are coming together again and their shadow looms and the ship
is about to be overwhelmed and crushed, but Juno and Pallas   690
descend from the sky in a sudden leap and land on the rocks,
and one holds on to the one and the other seizes the other,
as if they bulldogged a pair of oxen, holding their horns.
The sea, meanwhile, is seething, the water churning up sand
and the waves rushing in to fill the suddenly empty spaces
the rocks have left in their wake. The oarsmen row in a frenzy,
darting into that narrowing space between the closing
shapes that catch the poop's projection aft and crush
the vessel's transom. The Minyae cry aloud in alarm
for they think that this is the end, that the ship will founder and sink,   700
and the sickening noise rings in their ears of the shivered timbers,
but thanks to the gods in heaven, they seem to have somehow escaped,
and Tiphys is still there at the tiller, alive, unharmed,
and in control as, behind him, the cliffs sluice water down
their rocky faces. The men are rowing as hard as ever,
and they keep up their pace as they pass the Rheba's mouth, where they feel
their leaden arms' complaint and at last allow them to rest.
Their chests heave from exertion, and the men are giddy, exhausted,
but delighted, too, to be still alive and to be still breathing.
Thus it must have been when Hercules returned   710

with Theseus from Avernus and, back in the light, they embraced.
  But Jason is not altogether relieved and explains his concern,
saying, "Suppose that we get there, reaching the Phasis at last,
and suppose that the people of Colchis are welcoming, courteous, decent,
and the fleece is ours for the asking. How do we then get back
and pass through these terrible moving mountains a second time?"
What he doesn't know is the rocks no longer move, that Jove
· has ordered that fate's immutable law be imposed — that once
a ship has somehow passed between them and into the open
720 sea that lies beyond, they remain fixed in their places.
  Those waters of that distant sea on which they were sailing
gazed at the ship with amazement, never before having seen one.
And on their part, the crew looked out at the low-lying shore and at people
and kings of whom they had heard only in vague reports.
But there it was, the coast where the sevenfold mouth of the Hister
pours forth into the sea. Where can one find such a thing
anywhere else? The Aegean shoreline has many fine prospects,
and one can admire imposing Tyrrhenian headlands. The Syrtes'
sandbanks are most impressive. But here are mighty rivers
730 of much of the earth that flow to meet this sea: the Tanais,
the yellow Tyres, Hypanis, and the gently winding Novas.
There are large Maeotian bays where the waters, shallow and sheltered,
freeze when the winter Bear lopes across the sky, and the waves
harden into a rolling plain that lies white with snow,
Europe in one direction and Asia's expanses across
where the shore curves in the shape of a Scythian archer's bow.
The weather is harsh and cold and the sky is filled with clouds
so that even when spring returns the waters remain hard-frozen
to the equinox and beyond, well into May, when the Bull
740 returns to preside again in its place in heaven's vault.
  Now the ship draws abeam of the land of the Mariandyni,
and Echion again sets out to bear the message
of Jason's greeting, for here, if anywhere in these regions,
the names of the chosen heroes of Greece may not be unknown.
Lycus, the king, is delighted to hear that the Greeks have arrived
and he hastens down to the shore to invite the crew to his palace,
the walls of which are hung with trophies of war from engagements
with hated Bebrycia. To these King Lycus points as he speaks:

"It is no mere chance that has brought you here to our shore, but divine
fate. You are foes of my foe, and therefore my friends, whom I welcome   750
with thanks and my pledge of alliance. We have known Amycus' vileness
ourselves: he killed my brother on that blood-soaked stretch of beach.
In a passion for vengeance, our troops were about to set forth for battle
when the news arrived that the sea was bearing your vessel hither.
That man was a tyrant, a monster, subhuman or superhuman,
and covered in gore and corruption. I do not complain at the news
of his death, which I had expected with my own hands to impose.
Instead, I rejoice and thank you. For blood he shed, his blood
is also shed, as is right and just." "Was it then your beacon
we saw from far out to sea?" asks Jason. And Lycus nods.   760
And Jason presents his shipmate, the hero and son of Jove.
"This is Pollux," he says, "who vanquished the man you hated."
Lycus is all but speechless with admiration and thanks
but he orders the banquet prepared to honor their common gods
by whose decree the wicked Bebrycian has been undone.
They will celebrate together and offer their prayers of thanksgiving.

Book V

For the brave men of the *Argo*, dawn broke with a joyless
light that revealed how Idmon had sickened that night and died,
as Jason remembered Phineus said that he would — which meant
that his other dire predictions might also prove to be true.
But he kept his concerns to himself as he uttered words of praise
and respect for the friend who was suddenly taken this way from their midst
and he offered as a farewell tribute a fine embroidered cloak
to be used as a shroud, while Lycus granted a plot of ground
in which to inter the corpse. In tears, Mopsus, his colleague
10   and fellow prophet, fetched from the ship's hold Idmon's armor
while a squad of men felled trees from the woods for the funeral pyre
and others decked the dead man's head with the augur's wreaths
and prognosticator's ribbons and set him up on his bier
in sadness for him and for every mortal, including themselves.

Their tears are not yet dry from their prayers for Idmon, when Tiphys,
racked with fevers and chills, shudders with rigors. The men
are appalled and in fear they pray to heaven to spare their shipmate
on whom they all depend: "Give ear, Apollo, O mighty
god who shoots from afar to send diseases to men
20   but who also can heal. Revive the guttering flame of the life
of this good man, whose skill we need for our venture. Approving
of what we do, help us continue. We pray you: heal him."
They might as well have spoken to empty air, for Tiphys'
fate was not at all changed. The crew were afraid, like children
whose father lies on his deathbed, failing from moment to moment,
and the little ones wail as grief and dread are warring within them.

Thus do the Minyae watch in this fateful time and hope
that Tiphys may yet be spared, but clammy death advances,
its appetite whetted from having already taken Idmon—
beside whose pyre there now is another on which they set   30
the stiffened corpse of their second shipmate with tears and gifts
for the flames to devour. The crew in their hearts have a sinking feeling
as if at sea their vessel is about to go down in flames.
What the men feel, their chief, the son of Aeson, expresses,
as he puts his spirit's groan of torment into his words:
"What have we done? Why have the gods now turned against us?
For what crime are we punished? Here, ashore, and in safety,
we are stricken nonetheless. Have we men to spare? Can our crew
afford such grievous losses? A pair of funeral pyres
is here for the two who are carried off by sickness. And I   40
abandoned Hercules! Tiphys' skill, and Idmon's,
we need, and Hercules' strength and the valor he always displayed
in the tribulations to which his stepmother's hatred put him.
Tiphys stood on the poop with his hand on the tiller, plotting
our course by the stars he knew, the Pleiades and the Bear,
but who shall now take his place to guide us? Who will allow me
to sleep at night, assured that all things will be well
as long as he's standing watch? Is this the reward he has earned
for all those nights when he kept his tired eyes wide open?
Now they are closed, and we are far off course from the Phasis,   50
but perhaps his shadowy spirit will hover about us, a shade
that will share its knowledge and warn our helmsmen of brewing storms."
Thus he spoke as the flames died down to leave bare bones
of both the men, and Jason remarked on them as he stared
in sadness at all that remained of his comrades, "At least they're together.
This may be the end of the earth, remote and lonely, but they
are joined in the tomb forever in death as they were in life
on the ship." The men assembled their relics and heaped up the living
turf for the burial mound in which Jason then placed their combined
ashes, which he entrusted to Lycus' care and protection.   60
        Gloomy they were, and concerned, for on which of their number now
could they rely to guide their ship in Tiphys' place?
Ancaeus offered himself, and Nauplius volunteered,
but the wood of the ship spoke and at fate's prompting suggested

Erginus. The others returned to their rowing benches. Imagine
a bull who now has become the lord of the herd and struts
and paws the earth in his triumph, for he is the honored alpha
to whom all love and honor rightly belong — and Erginus
steps up thus to assume command at the vessel's helm,
70   for the night is clear and it shows the polestar high in the sky.
They weigh the anchors at bow and stern and the prow is moving
and they separate from the shore of that land of sickness and death.

The wind is fair from the south and the *Argo* is passing by
the Bithynian promontory and Callichoros, the site
of extravagant Bacchic revels — those tales people tell are true,
for this is the shore where the god once washed those switches that dripped
with the blood of his devotees. From Egypt's farthest reaches
he arrived here to arouse his votaries' passions with sounds
of crashing cymbals and flutes as they danced with the vine-leaf wreaths
80   askew on their heads in a frenzy that Thebes would learn on Cithaeron.

Fame, meanwhile, had spread the word of the vessel's progress
to the world's remotest regions and even the realms below
where the shades took their wan delight in reports of their heirs' achievements
and the news that the new sea was added now to the lanes
on which men's ships could venture, the dreadful Cyanean rocks
having been passed and that barrier breached. There are smiles that appear
even on their ghostly faces at valor's reward,
not that it makes much difference to any of them, except
for Sthenelus, who now goes forth, he who had joined
90   in the fight Hercules waged with the Amazon forces. That hero
had buried his comrade here on the beach clad in full armor
that he still wore, and it flashed in the sunlight again as he rose
from that funeral mound at the water's edge to peer out at the vessel.
The sun-shot waves were adazzle, gleaming with light as the clouds
opened to show the sailors a glimpse of Sthenelus' grave
ghost that after a grief-stricken moment dove back to the dark
depths below. Mopsus considered the eerie vision
and then, as he understood it, pointed to show his companions
that lonely grave on the beach. He veiled his head in mourning
100   and poured a libation of wine to appease the restless spirit,
while Orpheus took up his lyre and intoned the dolorous chant
to soothe the shade, whose name he awarded now to this coast.

The wind freshens. The Paphlagonian coast slips by
and the mouth of Parthenius Tiphys had hoped to see, but the Fates
denied him this. The river is sacred: the goddess Diana
is as partial to it as she is to her mother's Inopus on Delos.
They are moving along and making excellent progress. The ridge
of Cromna slips beneath the horizon, and wooded Cytorus,
and the island of Erythia then disappears astern.
The sky darkens and night comes on as they pass Carambis'   110
rocky point and the looming shadow of Sinope, rich
in association, for here the nymph of that name, Asopus'
daughter, eluded Jove's ardent advances. He offered
whatever gift she might name, never expecting her answer:
"Virginity." (To Halys, the god of the Asian river,
she gave the same reply, and Apollo as well, they say.)
    And now the Minyae's numbers are bolstered as Fortune presents
new recruits in the persons of three heroes who followed
Hercules to these distant regions, where they were stranded.
Autolycus, Phlogius, and Deileon see the Pelasgian ship,   120
run to the water's edge, and beg to sign on for the voyage.
Jason, of course, is delighted to see the empty benches
filled again and at once accepts the three new rowers.
Halys they pass, and Iris' gently meandering stream,
and the Thermodon, whose current extends far out to sea.
This river, rich with spoils, is sacred to Gradivus Mars
and to it the Amazons offer their prizes of war, the axes
and other such weapons and even the horses they take from their foes
when they come home in their triumph from having bested the best
of the Medians or the Massegetae, whose captives they lead   130
in chains behind their chariot wheels as they enter the Caspian
gate of their proud city, for these are the daughters of Mars.
The Greeks, paying attention to Phineus' warning, give wide
berth to the Amazons' coast and pass by far out to sea.
Jason, meanwhile, turns to the new shipmates to ask them
to tell of their battles and all their adventures and say what it was
that left them here on this shore of Mars, and they tell their story
to which the Minyae attend with saddened hearts as they hear
how these three fought with the Amazon horde, and which one dropped
the reins and fell from her cart and into the river that bore her,   140

more dead than alive, on its way to the sea, and which one fled
from the field, dropping her shield as she ran away, and her quiver,
although Hercules caught up and pierced her side with his lance;
and Anger and Mars, their father, responded, urging the women
to dry their tears and fight. Wielding an axe, their leader
stood her ground as a Fury drove her on and she rallied
the others to counterattack, and her baldric blazed in the sunlight.

   It was night and they heard in the darkness from caves deep in the earth
the sounds of the Chalybes' labors with hammer and anvil to fashion
150   implements for the bloody harvests of Gradivus Mars,
the scourge of the earth, for before these people had given us weapons,
Hatred was ineffectual, Anger was feeble, and even
Revenge was slow and without the means to inflict real harm.
The heroes then pass the rock of the Genetaean Jove
and the Tibarene's green lake, where they say that, when women give birth,
their husbands lie down in bed in couvade, and the women deliver
and, as soon as they can, get up to tend their distressed menfolk.
They pass the Mossynians' land, and the natives look out in amazement
to see the sails of a ship. The Macrones, too, are astonished
160   and peer out from their lofty perches. The nomad tribes
of Byzeres live there, too, on the shores where Philyra roamed,
that nymph whom Saturn had wooed in the form of a mighty stallion.

   And now they round the point and see that forbidding bay
where the Caucasus mountain rises abruptly into the frigid
northern air where Prometheus suffers in dreadful anguish.
On the same day as the Minyae appear, their comrade also
arrives, Hercules, sent to the aid of the fettered Titan.
He hacks at the bonds and chips at the ice and bedrock to tear
the bolted shackles free. With his great strength, he succeeds
170   in dislodging the mountain's structure, and the avalanche that follows
resounds as mighty trees are uprooted and rock and scree
plummet down to dam the riverbeds in their hollows
and block their course to the sea. The crash is intimidating,
and one might have supposed that Jove had arisen, or Neptune,
to shake the world's foundation. The entire Black Sea sloshes
and sends forth enormous waves that break on distant beaches
as far away as Georgia. The Minyae quake in their vessel,
worried lest the Cyanean rocks have come in pursuit.

They hear the clang of iron and the further groan of the rocks
that Hercules dislodges as he works to relieve the Titan   180
—although they have no idea what this could be. Who knew?
Who could imagine the shipmate of whom they all despaired
of ever seeing again was close at hand? They proceed
looking up at the lofty crags and ice-covered rocks
strewn on the beach. Overhead an enormous dying bird
describes a lazy circle. Its shadow passes. They see,
or think they see, a rain of blood that falls from its claws.

The setting sun has touched the waves in a reddish black
when the last light of the day shows the weary rowers the mouth
of the broad River Phasis where fresh water pours to the sea.   190
They exult and exchange congratulations as they think back
over all the places they've been and the people they've seen on their way
here to Colchis. And Juno and Pallas, high in the sky,
let go the reins and halt their flying chariots' steeds.

Jason turns the vessel's prow upstream, inland,
and the rowers sweep with their oars against the river's current,
but he sees on the bank a ring of poplars around a mound,
the tomb of his kinsman Phrixus, beside which is a statue
in marble that represents his unfortunate sister Helle,
caught between her wicked stepmother Ino on one side   200
and the cruel sea on the other, and clinging in fear to the ram
that flew through the air. He bids the rowers take him ashore.
Setting the anchor cables, he disembarks as boldly
as if they were home in port in the shipyard of Pagasae.
Bearing the sacramental wine in a heavy bowl,
he approaches the tomb and its altar and pours out the libation,
addressing the ghosts of the dead: "Phrixus, hear me, your kinsman.
I pray you be my guide in this enterprise. Protect us
and help us now that we've reached this land, having survived
the perils of the trackless seas we have crossed. Remember   210
your countrymen in kindness, and favor your kinfolk.
And you, too, my lady, at whose empty tomb I stand,
a goddess now of the sea, be gracious to us and help us
now and on our return when we venture again on your waves.
When shall that golden fleece sail again past Sestus,
perhaps to recognize that unfortunate stretch of water?

And you, O woods and shores of Colchis, welcome us now
and lead us to that sacred tree where the glittering fleece
hangs. And you, O Phasis, child of potent Jove,
220 accept and allow Minerva's vessel to travel between
your banks on your tranquil current. Appropriate gifts I promise
at shrines that I shall erect in your honor when I get home —
statues commanding the reverence we pay to the Enipeus
or the Inachus whose god lolls in his golden cave."
Thus does Jason speak, and the ship, as if it has heard him,
turns without the touch of a man's hand on its helm
to face the river's mouth and the open sea beyond it.
A fortunate omen, and Jason cries aloud to his vessel,
"For your promise that we shall return, we offer our fervent thanks."
230 He then orders the men to fetch their arms from the poop
and prepare the wine of Bacchus and the grain of Ceres to offer
as gifts to the gods as the Minyae ask for strength and good fortune
in the trials they know await them along the green banks of the river.

    And now, O goddess, begin in a new and different mode
to tell the story of Jason, the Thessalian chieftain whose deeds
you with your own eyes witnessed. Assist my feeble powers
and give my speech that strength it needs to describe the madness;
the excess of the princess; the dark bargain they made;
the evil that caused the planks of the vessel she rode aboard
240 to shudder under her feet; the supernatural contest
in that faraway arena . . . It all rises up before me,
intimidating and all but defying reason itself.
But first, I ought to explain how Aeëtes, son of the Sun,
through his bad faith deserved whatever he got and worse,
betrayed as he would be and deserted by his daughter,
for this is the start of the story, when Phrixus, having grown old,
died in the Scythian town of Aea where King Aeëtes,
his father-in-law, lived and ruled. There appeared in the sky
pricked out in stars a ram like the one that had carried Phrixus,
250 the fleece of which had turned to gold and was now displayed
in the grove sacred to Mars, where it shone on a tall oak tree.
One night the ghost of Phrixus appeared in the king's dream
to speak in a thundering voice and strike fear into his heart:
"Once you welcomed me in, a fugitive; you allowed me

to settle; you gave me your daughter Chalciope as my bride.
Considering this, I warn you that grief and ruin await you
and all your kingdom if ever my golden fleece be stolen
out of that somnolent grove of the god. And a further warning:
your daughter, Medea, who now is a devotee of Diana
and leads the ritual dances, let her accept a suitor   260
from a foreign land and leave her home and her father's kingdom."
He spoke no more but seemed in this dream to extend his hand
in which he held that shining fleece of gold—and its gleam
shimmered across the ceiling in erratic play. The king
was startled, awoke, arose from his bed, and addressed his father,
the god of the sun, whose car would soon appear from the east.
"Father," he said, "I pray you, all-seeing guardian god,
be gracious to me and protect me, watching over my kingdom.
Be vigilant ever and warn me what subjects of mine or strangers
conspire against me. Whatever treacherous plots there may be,   270
keep me alert and prepared. And you, Gradivus, hear me,
on whose sacred oak that fleece glitters. Protect it and keep it
safe always, your arms prepared to clash at the clarion's
sound to which your voice responds, ringing out in the darkness."
He had scarcely finished speaking when a serpent appeared, the god's
clear omen, arrived from the Caucasus' heights to coil
and encircle that grove, its head upheld and looking toward Greece.
The king, therefore, is persuaded and takes all proper precautions
against those perils Phrixus' ghost described—and Medea,
though still a little girl, is betrothed to Albania's prince.   280
     And Apollo, the god who warns the cities of men with omens
and threatening signs, brings portents of trouble to come to the priests,
who caution the king and bid him give up that fatal fleece
and let it carry catastrophe back to the land of the Greeks,
but the son of the Sun is stubborn as he ponders within his bosom
the priests' and Phrixus' warnings, nor does he consult with his people,
for Asian tyrants can never trust in the men around them,
all of whom they assume to be traitors, biding their time.
Perses, Aeëtes' brother, next in line to the throne,
urges him to accept and act on his priests' good counsel   290
and the others at court concur, but the king is only enraged
and rises up from his throne to bid the lot begone,

and they scatter, run for their lives as the king considers how Perses
was the man to whom they threw their support, and him he attacks,
swinging the royal sword, but he only wounds him. Escaping,
Perses has no other choice, and in desperation assembles
the forces of discontent that are always ready to muster,
and Rumor is his ally. Their horde moves toward the city,
thousands of them, and there before the walls they halt,
300   stopped for the moment, and inside and out there is fear and confusion.
The next day, there's a lull if not quite a truce, and they tend
their wounded and burn their dead. And this is the moment when fate
has ordained for Jason's ship to arrive at Aea's harbor.

      It was night, that compassionate time when weary earth can recover
and refresh itself. In heaven, Juno and Jupiter's daughter
Minerva talked and considered the likeliest way to proceed.
Minerva began by asking, "Which side ought we to favor?
You see how the men of Colchis struggle in battle, contesting
who should have the power and sit on the throne, Aeëtes
310   or Perses? To which should we give our aid?" And Juno replied,
"For you the question is only which side we should fight on,
for fighting is what you love, and you shall not be disappointed.
Your aegis will shine on the field as your steeds draw your battle car.
On Aeëtes' side, I think. That king, I admit, is a snake,
an unreliable man and mean, and he will refuse
the request the Minyae make, but we shall have other resources
that we can then bring to bear." Pallas was not unhappy.
"Whatever you say," she answered, "so long as we're on the same side,
and so long as we keep in mind that our goal in the end is Jason's
320   safe return to Greece and that of the ship we made
that must one day ride at anchor, proud in its harbor at home."

      Thus did the higher powers plot for the glory of men's
grand achievements, while they who were quite unaware below
were fretful and all but dismayed in the gloom of night. The Minyae
had reached the banks of the Phasis and passed through the clashing rocks,
but none of it mattered. The real work yet remained before them,
the king's perilous city so full of the schemes of men
in the depths of which their venture's outcome hung in doubt.
Jason's thoughts were skittish and his moods constantly changing,
330   as plans came into being that he then revised and discarded

as new ideas crossed his mind. Homer describes how Jove
flings lightning bolts and darkens the Pleiades with clouds
as rain falls, or snow, and the thunder claps and the plains'
features are shrouded in white as he opens the gates of war,
and men and nations can feel their destinies now approaching:
in such a way does the chief feel in his heart that storming,
wind-whipped, and icy cold to make even bravery groan
under the weight of the hours that he must endure until dawn
when the face of the truth shall at last be revealed. In such condition
did Jason turn to his silent men, who stared at the ground: 340
"This glorious undertaking on which we have fixed our hopes
and prayers, this splendid adventure here in the wilds of Asia—
even the thought of it daunted all men of ages past—
is now at hand and in reach. The journey's dangers are past,
and we have survived the snares of the shifting tides and the waves.
We have come to Aeëtes' city, which people said was beyond
the ends of the earth. The dawn will break in the east to reveal
the dwelling places of mortals. There we shall take our chances
as we try our wits with his. We'll make our request and see
what he says and then what he does. My guess is that he'll say yes   350
and promise to give what we're asking. But don't be surprised or dismayed
if he should refuse us or even insult us and send us away.
If that happens, then we will do what we have to do,
for, one way or another, we shall bring the fleece back home.
It's only when times are tough that the tough can show what they're made of."
His words were done, and the men turned to the business at hand,
picking by lot the nine of the crew who would go with Jason
into the foreigners' town. Without delay, they set out
at the break of dawn on the royal road that crosses the plain.
      By chance, Medea had woken early that morning, roused   360
from her nightmares of dismal portent. She left her bed and was walking
east to the riverbank to wash their taint away
to keep those terrible dreams from ever being fulfilled.
A maiden, asleep in her room, what business had she with these
ghastly visions in which, stepping forth from Hecate's shrine
in the holy grove, she had had a vertiginous sense of abyss
on every side, and water, a large body of water
that somehow cut her off from her father? Her brother pursued her,

but then it was murk and terror, with blood on her hands, and children
370 weeping in fear, and she was shedding her own bitter tears.
From this she had managed to wake, and she set out at once for the Phasis
with a few of her court attendants. They looked like a scene from a pageant
of Proserpine on Hymettus' flowery ridge with her playmates,
those nymphs with whom she romped with the visiting goddesses, Pallas
and, hand in hand, Diana, just before the dread moment
when the earth opened up at her feet to reveal Avernus' dismal
caverns, to which she was fated. That's what Medea resembled
making her way to the river with Hecate's pair of torches
and wearing her badge of office, the priestess' sacred fillets.
380 She was innocent, still, and had not the first thought of betraying
her unfortunate father, her native country, her kin, and her people,
when she saw at a distance the band of men coming up from the river.
She stopped and in apprehension turned to her nursemaid to ask
"Who are these strangers marching in our direction? What
do they want with us? Why are they dressed that way? Should we run?
Is there somewhere safe we can hide?" Her nursemaid, Henioche, answered,
reassuring the girl whose honor and safety she guarded:
"They are, from the look of them, Greeks. See how their garments are dyed
all those gaudy colors. Phrixus wore such clothing.
390 And they do not threaten violence or mean us harm, for they carry
the olive branches of peace and they wear the sacred ribbons
of devotees of the gods." While the nurse is still speaking, Juno
also exerts herself to make the young girl receptive.
Jason's exertions have worn him down and the weight of his cares
as the ship's commander have sapped his strength and affected his looks,
which the goddess now improves, shedding upon him the glow
of perfect youth and robust health and making him gorgeous,
unsurpassed in his beauty by even the handsomest Minyae,
Talaus and Mopsus, or even Castor and Pollux, whose hair
400 seemed almost to twinkle . . . Think how on autumn nights
when Sirius shines in the heavens, its brightness is such as to dim
the other stars in the sky, and here on earth the fields
are parched from the heat it brings and the riverbeds languish and thirst:
such was the glorious brilliance of Jason that struck Medea,
astonishing her. She is speechless, stupefied, as she gazes
only at him. His companions, the other Greek heroes, fade

into the dull surround of a colorless boring world,
while he stands vivid and clear. For him, meanwhile, Medea,
commanding, queenly, is lovely. Addressing her, he asks
if she is a goddess come down for a time from Olympus to visit   410
mortals on earth. "The ritual torches your nymphs in attendance
carry contribute nothing to your own numinous brightness
as you wander here with your escorts along this Caucasian river.
But if I am somehow mistaken, and you are a mortal whose home
is here on earth, then your parents I'm sure must take great pride
in having you now as their daughter, as someday that fortunate man
who bears you away as his bride will also rejoice and be happy.
Meanwhile, O noble lady, I ask you to grant your favor
and aid to a band of princes of Greece who have crossed the sea
to seek the house of the king. Lead us, I pray, to your lord   420
and let us know the correct customs and proper mode
of address we ought to employ. Heaven has intervened,
sending you here to cross our path at this critical moment.
Ignorant as we are, we rely on your good advice,
and something within me tells me to trust in your goodwill."
      In those words Jason spoke. And the maiden stood in silence,
afraid or merely shy in the presence of men who were strangers,
but, overcoming her maidenly diffidence, she managed
an answer: "My father is King Aeëtes, whose palace you seek
in the city just over there. There's a path you can easily follow.   430
I'll send a girl to guide you. It's better that way than the roads,
on all of which there are mobs of rebellious men in arms."
Having said this she turned and went on her way to the river
to perform those cleansing rites (which, in her case, were useless)
she hoped might expunge those dreams and avoid their terrible omen.
      Jason, meanwhile, in haste set out along that pathway
with one of Medea's maidens guiding the Greeks into town
while Juno sent a mist to envelop the band of Minyae
and keep them from being seen, lest any word of the coming
of strangers reach the ear of Aeëtes before their arrival.   440
They were negotiating the crowded streets of the city
when their guide, Medea's attendant, explained to them that the king
would soon be passing this way to visit the shrine of his father,
Phoebus Apollo, where every day he hears the complaints

and receives his people's petitions and prayers and renders judgments,
his own wisdom inspired by his father's awesome presence.

     They entered the gorgeous temple and stared in awe at the god,
whose statue seemed to float in light that gleamed from the walls
, that showed in rich detail a picture of Atlas, the Titan,
450   who stood with his feet in the ocean and on his broad shoulders held
the huge bowl of the sky, across which Apollo's steeds
drew his shining car and illuminated the cosmos.
Behind him with smaller wheels, the Pleiades' chariots followed
and the Hyades trailed behind them, raindrops making their hair
glisten as if with diamonds. Delighted, Jason examined
each of these works of art and then he admired the doors
on which were carved the stories of the founding of Colchis' race:
their first king, Sesostris, came from Egypt to fight
the fierce native Getae; dismayed by the bloody slaughter
460   the Egyptians fell back, some to Thebae and others to the banks
of the River Phasis and there they founded the kingdom of Colchis.
In the frigid north they dwell, longing for sun-bathed Pharos
and Arsinoë's wealth and ease, while they fight the cold, and wear,
instead of Egyptian robes, the warmer Sarmatian trousers.
Another panel shows the pursuit by frenzied Phasis
across the local hills of the terrified nymph, Aea;
as she runs, she is shooting useless arrows, but none of them stops
the lustful god, who is gaining, for she has begun to tire.
And then, in the next scene, he has caught her and bound her feet
470   and he drags her down beneath his rolling waves as his prize.
Meanwhile his sisters, the poplar trees on the hillsides, weep,
but not for her. Instead, they shed their amber tears
for Phaethon, fallen out of the runaway car he has driven
to land as a charred cinder in the Eridanus' waters,
while Tethys gathers the fragments of the yoke and the axletree
and frees Pyroeis, trapped in the traces, who snorts in fear—
nor for himself but his master, burdened down now by grief.
On another panel, Vulcan had shown in a bas-relief
his prophecy now on the point of being fulfilled—the golden
480   fleece and the expedition Achaea would mount to fetch it.
There is the axe and the timber near Pagasae where the *Argo*
was built, and the captain boarding and beckoning all his crew.

There they are at sea, the only vessel to venture
so far from land with the goddess filling their sails with a gentle
but steady wind from the south, and dolphins leap to the song
in the Thracian mode that sets the tempo for burly oarsmen.
And there, at the mouths of Phasis, are people of Colchis in fear
as they watch their princess abscond while her parents, left behind,
wail in their grief and rage. Then, in the final panels,
in a faraway city somewhere between two bodies of water,   490
is a marriage scene, with torches waving and people dancing
and a groom proud of his bride . . . But something is terribly wrong.
It appears that he has abandoned another wife, for the Furies
watch from the palace roof, and the first wife, in her chamber,
prepares in her hatred a deadly gift of a crown and a poisoned
robe, and her face is contorted in anger or woe or both.
The penultimate scene is the rival, adorned at her country's altars
when the robe's venom has started to work and the house is in flames.
These were the images Vulcan had made for Apollo's temple
though no one in Colchis knew what their dark meaning might be   500
or who it could be in that last panel whom wingèd dragons
bear through the air while their claws are dripping murder and blood,
but they comprehend enough to turn away in dread.
    A similar horror grips the brave hearts of the Minyae
and holds them in its spell as the son of the Sun approaches
in panoply to enter the shrine of his godly father.
Beside him marches his son Absyrtus, a promising lad
worthy of his grandsire and deserving a better future
than what fate holds in store. Next is Albanian Styrus,
the newly arrived prince and prospective son-in-law,   510
whose marriage has been postponed until the war is concluded.
After him, Phrontis and Argus, of Aeolus' line, and their brother
Melas. (These three and Cytisorus, the adept hunter, are sons
of the exile Phrixus.) Following close on these were the nobles,
generals, princes, and men of the senate to whom the land
had given its recognition and honor. Choosing his moment,
Jason gives his comrades the signal and all together
they burst forth from their cloud in a sudden dazzle of glory.
The people of Colchis, astonished, gather about them to ask
who they are, and whence they have come, and what they want.   520

Jason waits them out and then, when their murmur subsides
and he sees that he has their attention, addresses their monarch, saying:
"Sire, Hyperion's son, the gods have commanded me here
in the first ship to cross the vast breadth of the seas
on our great quest. I come, as Phrixus did, from Greece,
from Thessaly, of which I am sure he must have spoken.
We are here before you, having survived the many hazards
of sea and land. I am Phrixus' kin, for we both descend
from Cretheus' line and Aeolus'. And before them, from Jove and Neptune,
530   out of the nymph Salmonis. I did not flee my homeland
as Phrixus did, from his father's sacrificial altar,
though it was not my own idea to journey all this way,
to visit one whose fame extends as far as Greece.
It was more than the honor and pleasure of meeting you that moved me
to defy the monsters that dwell in the deeps and those clashing rocks.
King Pelias, who reigns over one of the richest lands
beneath your father's orbit, with many bustling towns
along the ever-flowing rivers of fertile hillsides,
commanded me to come here, much as Sthenelus, son
540   of Perseus and the king of Argos, imposed upon
Hercules those arduous labors. Kings can be cruel,
and their subjects must somehow endure, as Hercules did,
and I, in a lesser way, who am bound to try my best.
The charge that Pelias gave me was to journey here to fetch
the fleece of the golden ram. I do as I am bidden,
the king's obedient servant — which you, a king, must count
as deserving of approbation. My hope is to find a response
from you that is different and better than what Pelias expects
and even wants, which is warfare and the cruel shedding of blood.
550   Had I seen no other way, I could have come with an army,
with the help of princes of Ossa and Pindus, who offered ships
and fighting men, as many as Perseus had when he came here
many long years ago. Reason and justice are better,
and decency, on which I rely as I ask, in the name
of your friendship with Phrixus, that we join our hands as comrades.
The other and unattractive choice is for me to behave
as I was forced to do on Phrygian beaches and then
in Bebrycia's hostile land, where for their disrespect

to a visitor I contrived to impose a severe correction.
Honor we meet with honor, and threats and affronts we answer   560
in kind, as the sons of gods whose vessel Minerva blesses
and considers her own. We have only just arrived in Colchis,
the goal of all our efforts and prayers, and we are delighted
to be here and see for ourselves that splendor of your court
and person that earns you fame throughout the civilized world.
Do not begrudge the Minyae that gift of glory they seek.
What we request is only what is ours by right,
and yet we do not demand but pray . . . and we trust in you
to give as you would have given to Phrixus and to his house,
to which we will carry this prize. In return, in token of thanks   570
and praise, we offer gifts we have carried over the seas:
a rich cloak, bright red from the dyes of Taenarian vats;
a bridle; a sword whose hilt is a dazzle of gems — these all
were parts of my father's regalia. The cloak, my mother wove.
The bridle is that of the Lapiths, who invented them and still
manufacture the best in the world. Let us exchange
these gifts and pledge our friendship, and let my master know
his expectations are wrong and that here in the Caucasus' wilds
I have found in the king and people refinement and laudable kindness."

    While Jason spoke, the other listened, his face a mask   580
that barely concealed the fires that smoldered within his breast.
As a wave that rolls in the ocean and seems, far off from the land,
a mere swell but closer will grow to a towering breaker,
so his anger enlarged in the depths of his heart as he thought
what a foolish, insolent, cheeky fellow this was to expect
that the nonsense he was spouting might have any chance of success.
He was convinced that his first mistake was in welcoming Phrixus
years before, when he could have taught the whole world a lesson
and made of him an example of the fierceness of Scythian ways.
Shaking his head, he mocked the young man's vacuous mouthings.   590
The words in his mind were clear: "What drivel is this, what raving,
to ask for the golden fleece?" But he checked himself as he thought
of that ancient oracle's warning that burned in his memory still.
Why had fortune dealt him a blow on a blow with Perses
and now this Thessalian ship with its crew of thugs? Had his luck
turned? Were the Fates demanding that the fleece be given away?

Under necessity's burden, he framed a more politic answer,
thinking that he might contrive to enlist their aid in the war.
Therefore with gentle and peaceful words he answered Jason:
600 "You come at a bad time, when a powerful foe assails me.
My brother has turned against me, envious, greedy for power,
and attacking in force. You come, sir, with opportune offers of friendship
and advancing claims of kinship. Join with me, then, in this struggle,
and stake your stranger's claim to the glory of martial exploits,
the chance of which is ever attractive to hearts of heroes.
Once the battle is ended with both of us as the victors,
I will bestow upon you the fleece as your share of the spoils,
and that will be only a portion of what you shall then have deserved."
Jason, lacking in guile and trusting in what men say,
610 replied to the king: "For this difficult task, it seems we are sent here
by fate. What we have already suffered at sea is behind us,
and of no account. Let us face what the day proposes. Your struggle
is ours, and with blood shall your brother pay for the trouble he's
               caused you—
and us, too, who are for a brief time thus delayed."
Saying this, he dispatches Castor back to the vessel
to inform the rest of the men what the king of Aea has said,
for he knows how heavy the burden must be of their anxious hours
of waiting for news. At the ship, when the men see him approaching,
trepidation seizes their hearts, and they call out to Castor,
620 "Speak, Jupiter's son! Say what our prospects are
and what are our chances of ever seeing our homes again."
To this, Castor replies to thickly clustered Achaeans,
"Aeëtes is not at all the savage that rumor portrays,
but a civilized fellow. He does not deny us the golden fleece.
He says he will grant our request, but first he asks our help
now that he is attacked by hostile forces, and Jason
bids us arm and hurry to give that assistance. Our ship,
hidden here as it is from the city, is not in danger."
     They spring forward, those eager men whom no Eastern bowmen
630 could think of standing up to, and falling into formation
march off toward the battle, its dangers and chances of glory,
as the freshening breeze ripples the bright crests of their helmets
and the dull brown of the roadway blooms with the brilliant hues

of their various shields and the burnished metals glint sunshine
to make one think of the stars that gleam in the skies at night
to cover the earth with the priceless quilt of a queen's boudoir.
Aeëtes, the Sun's son, inspects the arriving troop
with a jaundiced eye, but then, as he thinks of his situation,
decides it is better to have such an enemy force as this
allied with him and within his palace walls than out there   640
opposed with that traitorous band. He puts on a cheerful face
and presides at a royal banquet with a great bowl of wine he offers
to Jason, who sits beside him to tell him the others' names
and the names of their fathers: These are Aeacus' sons, and those
are the children of Jove almighty. Jason also rehearses
the story of how they left the mighty Hercules
to wander the woods in his grief and torment, and gives him accounts
of their other trials and toils and adventures on land and sea.
He also asks the king to identify the others
who have come to fight in the war: "That fellow there, with the belt   650
with the fancy studs, and the squire with a strung bow, who are they?"
Aeëtes answers, "That one? He is called Carmeius.
And it is his habit always to have his weapon ready."
"And him, over there?" asks Jason. "Who is he with the cloak
embroidered in all those colors, and with perfumed oil in his hair?"
"Aron," Aeëtes tells him, "a wealthy man. His horsemen
splash themselves with cologne and reek of spice and saffron,
and curl their hair, as you see, but don't let yourself be fooled.
They're skillful fighters and tough. And that one in tiger skin
goes by the name of Campesus. And that one drinking his wine,   660
the one with the bushy beard that he can't help dribbling into,
he is called Odrussa." Jason takes all this in,
appraising each of these men, and Iaxartes, too,
whose loud mouth is foul with curses and violent threats
that one would think would offend the Olympian gods. But Aeëtes
assures his guest, "Those taunts and insults he's always spewing
are not just empty words, for he backs them up with a sword
and, at any time of the day or night, is ready to fight.
Even in coldest winter when their rivers freeze, the Getae
are worried lest he appear, and the Medes are jumpy and nervous   670
wondering where he may pass through one of their border outposts.

And the one near him is Latagus, and then on his right is Choaspes,
the son of the river god who survives in the field, men say,
by drinking the blood of his horses. But to name each person here
and explain who he is and where he is from would take all night.
Tomorrow you'll see for yourself when the troops are mustered, each
chief's colors and all their weapons — which ones shoot
with slings, and which rely on the javelin, and which
prefer to use bows and arrows. Imagine the splendid scene!
680 The Amazon Euryale, trampling dead and dying
and shrieking out in terrible glee as she waves her axe . . .
She is as dear to me as if she were my own daughter."
Grinning now in delight, he pours out wine from the bowl
to honor his godly father and the other Olympian gods
that they may look down with favor and grant success in battle,
survival of this ordeal, and the taste of victory's sweetness.

And now consider the picture of Mars, who comes onto the scene
trailing a huge cloud from the northern Getic caverns:
he sees at this banquet table the Argonauts and Aea's
690 old king, and they're laughing and drinking together. The fleece
that Jason has asked for is promised. How has this epic adventure
fizzled away to a trivial social occasion? The god
ascends to his father's palace high in the starry skies
and voices his bitter complaint to almighty Jove: "O sire,
what is become of battle? Are mortals to fight, or are we,
the gods, to plot and quarrel among ourselves to advance
whichever humans we favor? Pallas has gone too far.
Will you permit her excess that is neither just nor pleasing?
She has built a ship and sent it east to rob my grove
700 of its sacred fleece. She protects her chosen hero-thieves!
This cannot stand! Her wiles will end with my shrine despoiled
of Phrixus' treasure!" Here he turned and glared at Minerva.
"The kingdom of Colchis cannot claim your aid and favor!
You have put Aeëtes and Jason together as allies to fight
the rebel Perses! Better that you and I should go
to that glade where the trees are decked with gold and there take arms
and in single combat decide the quarrel between ourselves.
Let us descend together from heaven and you shall learn
what a mighty god you have dared offend! Those sacred branches

that are my sanctum I love, as other gods love their temples,   710
and mean to protect them against defilement. Mortals worship
outdoors there in the open with only a simple mound
beneath the trees, but in that place they know I hear
as well as the other gods are heard in their fancy structures
that vie with one another. Were I to plunder Mycenae's
heights or in Athens pilfer Cecrops' citadel's shrine,
there would be from Juno or Minerva loud complaint
and the shedding of copious tears. That isn't my style, but let them
remember who I am—the god of war—and fear me."
    Pallas, unafraid of the threats of Mars, defied him   720
and laughed in his face. "You think you are talking to Aloids or crude
Lapiths likely to be impressed by this kind of bluster?
What do you take me for? I am Minerva. Pallas!
And I should give up my aegis if I could be cowed by boasting.
I'll make you eat your words and hate your armor and trumpets
and all your paraphernalia. A fight between you and me?
You'd never live down the shame. You attack both me and your mother,
who regrets, I do not doubt, having ever brought forth
an ingrate and monster such as yourself. You accuse us of what
crime? How is it wrong to encourage a brave young man   730
who obeys the wicked command of his king to venture forth
on the sea as no man has before? How have we offended
by giving hope to a hero embarked on a noble adventure?
Bloody battles are all that you and that barbarous king
seem to understand, but other and better ways
to resolve disputes are at hand. Grant us the fleece, O sire,
and Jason will be on his way. If Mars insists on objecting,
shall we turn tail and flee in disgrace after having endured
so much to come to Colchis? He thinks he can take advantage
simply because I am female . . ." Here Mars jumped to his feet,   740
but before he could even begin his counterattack, his sire
cut him off: "Enough! This blather is too much to bear.
You get yourselves into trouble and then come here to complain.
Do whatever you want. Make wars and see where they get you.
Juno, Minerva, listen. I tell you now what will happen.
The Minyae are there, but let them not get involved in this war.
Perses at first will retreat, at least for a while, in fear

of the brave Greeks, who will leave, but then he'll renew his attack,
triumph over Aeëtes, and take the scepter and throne
750   to rule the land of Colchis until one day Medea
(having paid a dismaying price of atonement to fate) will return
to come to the aid of her helpless, agèd, and exiled father
and place on the throne his grandson, restoring his line once more.
This is what's going to happen. Go on and do what you will:
the result will not be changed." His words echoed away
in the great banqueting hall where harmony now was restored,
and then, from Olympus' peak, he sent down the stars of night
to adorn the cosmos. Apollo took up his lyre and strummed
to sing again the epic, the story of that Phlegraean
760   battle against the giants, while Ganymede passed around
the enormous wine-filled krater. At length, tired and happy,
they rose from their places and took their leave to their several dwellings.

Book VI

In the breast of vigilant Mars there is no respite: the passion
burns hot, as his mind contemplates which side
he ought in the end to favor of the forces drawn up for battle.
At length, he decides to appear in visible form to the rebels
so that he may destroy the Minyae and lay low Greece's heroes.
As his chariot hurtles along, the god holds his spear aloft,
that incontrovertible portent of war, and over the tents
of the Scythian horde the deity reins in his splendid chargers.
The Scythians bound from their couches and spring to arms while their chiefs
confer and attempt to decide what they may do, having heard   10
that Achaeans have come in a sacred vessel to claim the fleece
of Phrixus, and King Aeëtes has tricked them into alliance
so that now they will have to face Greeks in the coming battle.

They talk in the midnight hour while still there is time, and propose
to send to the Minyae a group of their warlords to carry the message
from Perses to try to warn them that Aeëtes is not to be trusted.
"Ask what foolish delusion could ever have blinded these Greeks,
and say that Perses has always counseled restoring the fleece
and urged that the king let go the skin of the sacred beast,
but he refused this advice, and this was what started the quarrel.   20
Let the Minyae consider on which side to look for friendship
and common interest. We are the ones they ought to trust,
or else they should just go home. But they must not commit to the cause
of a man whose word is worthless. One ought to avoid bloodshed
and refrain, whenever one can, from killing in strangers' fights.
Was it for this debacle that they sailed over all that ocean?

Why should they fight with men whom they do not hate or know?"
But even while Perses was telling his envoys what to say,
a peculiar golden glow lit up the field, and the weapons
30   seemed of their own accord to come to life and do battle
and trumpets that nobody blew blared forth signals to charge,
as Mars, overhead in his car, cried out: "Attack! Attack!
There is the enemy! Kill them! Kill!" And the troops from Colchis
rushed forward, and Perses' men swarmed forward to meet them,
and the plain was alive with weapons of every kind and loud
with the cries of the war god's voice ringing out in the throats of men.

     And now, O Muse, sing of the frantic deeds you beheld
in that cold and mountainous land and tell of the desperate striving
when Perses drove his Scythian horde, putting his hopes
40   and trust in the brave but mortal flesh of men and horses.
Who can name them or even count their numbers? Who,
if he were given a thousand thousand tongues, could begin
to retell those things that befell them there in those Asian steppes
and craggy hillsides, where manhood bleeds in battle and dies,
only to be replaced by the teeming womb of earth
beneath those pitiless constellations of northern skies?
O goddess, name, at least, the tribes that were there and their chieftains.

     The Alani and fierce Heniochi came with their leader Anausis,
he being resentful that Medea had been betrothed
50   to Albania's prince — he had no idea how lucky he was
not to have been so honored. That marriage bed he yearned for
was lumpy in ways he could never imagine, with terrible griefs
in store for the cities of men in faraway Achaea.
Next there come Bisalta's men with Colaxes, their chief.
He is an heir of the gods, having been begotten of Jove
in the green glades of Myrace near the mouths of the Tibisis River.
His mother was Hora, a nymph whose upper half was human
but below, instead of legs, were a pair of twining serpents.
The emblem of his men's shields was that of his mighty
60   father: the lightning bolt, repeated and then again
(just like the one the men of the Twelfth Legion now carry,
its flash dismaying the forces that meet with it out in the field).
Above these, in the design, was a pair of serpents in gold
in the likeness of those of Hora, and they faced each other, their mouths

open and tongues protruding to meet on a precious gem.
Then Auchus comes with his loyal minions, a thousand strong
and rich with Cimmerian wealth. This man was marked by the gods,
having been born with the hair on his head as white as a sage's.
Now in the ripeness of manhood, he has developed a bald spot,
but still from the triple band at his consecrated temples   70
the prophet's fillets dangle. The mighty Daraps is absent,
having sustained a wound in the Achaemenian conflict,
but he has sent Datis to take his place in the line of battle
and around him all the fierce Dandarid fighters, tough
from drinking the strong waters that flow in the Gerus River
and into the Lake of Byce. Anxur is there, and Sidon,
and his brother Rhadalus, and also a man who is named Phrixus,
the chief of the tribe that dwells by the banks of Acesinus.
A hind with golden horns and hide, rere-regardant,
is the emblem they bear before them advancing into battle —   80
from its high staff it seems to be looking back to the glade
of Diana's woodland in which it used to run free with its herd.
Syene was there as well with Hylaean fighting men, all
assembled in Perses' cause, having themselves endured
from Aeëtes ungentle treatment for which they could now extort
some payment of his atonement. Those arrows the king of Colchis
had discharged upward and into the loftiest treetops now
were about to descend to earth to put the archer in danger.
From distant Hyrcanian glens, Cyris had led his soldiers
to join with the wagon trains of the Coelaletaic nomads   90
who dwell in yerts, which are tents of hides they have stitched together.
Thus, their archers and lancers can fight all day, while their wives
are sitting at home nearby, and to them, each night, they return
as though they were still somewhere on the banks of the turbulent Tyra
at home, or perhaps on the lower slopes of Mount Ambenus
or Ophiusa, where poisonous herbs are reported to grow.
The Sindi are here, descendants of runaway Scythian slaves,
not brave perhaps — they appear to be always in fear of the whip —
but wily and certainly quick. Beside their encampment, Phalces
has bivouacked his boisterous crew of men in armor,   100
the Corallian tribesmen whose banners show pictures of porcupines.
They never use bugles but sing the songs of their fighting forebears

and with these stir their hearts to similar valorous deeds.
The Batarnae are there as well, with Teutagonus, their leader.
They fight with their horsemen and footmen intermixed, and their spears
are shorter-handled than most, and they throw them or use them as lances.
There are men from the icy Novas and Alazon, windswept
and frozen, and some from the Taras, and some from the steep banks
of the gentle Evarchus, where white swans paddle about on the stream.
110   And you, brave Ariasmenus, I would record for the ages'
      instruction and admiration, that mighty martial man
      who swept in triumph across the expansive plains of Asia,
      his chariots' wheels like scythes that left a cleared swath behind them.
      The Drancae are there, and the Caspian troops, who stream forth from
                  the lines
      with their packs of attack dogs, whose slavering jaws the trumpets summon
      to join with their masters in battle. (In death, they give these hounds
      the stately tombs and all the honors of war that heroes
      might hope to have earned.) A fearsome thing to behold, that pack
      of fighting canines with iron armor and feathered crests
120   as they bound across the field, baying aloud and belling
      like the dogs of the gates of hell or Hecate's terrible pack.
      Vanus is there, a seer, the leader of his contingent
      from Hyrcania's groves — there are now three generations to whom
      he had told of the Minyae's coming and the *Argo's* billowing sails.
      His keen wisdom has brought to Riphaea's soldiers' triumphs
      from Lagean meadows to Thebes in Egypt and distant Panchaia.
      Hiberia sent its squadrons of men with spears and lances
      in their colorfully gaudy getups. Otaces is one of their leaders,
      and with him are Latris and Neurus, the alleged child-molester,
130   and the Iazyges too have come, who never grow old. Instead,
      when they feel their strength has begun to diminish, they give their children
      swords and demand that they grant them a cleaner and quicker release
      from infirmity's dismal clutches — it's a terrible business, but splendid!
      The Mycaei are present — these troopers arrive with their hair doused
      with cologned pomades. The Cessae have checked in, too. (Arimaspus,
      their chief, will later establish his name in the mining of gold
      and silver, but has not yet the vaguest idea what wealth
      awaits the pick and shovel below his homeland's surface.)
      Auchates is there with his men, who are skilled in the lariat's use

and can bring down a horse or cow or an infantryman with a deft   140
flick of the wrist and an easy throw of the spinning rope.
Whom have I failed to mention? The Thyrsagetai, who march
to the beat of the drums they carry, and they trail great rawhide capes
and deck their spear-shafts with flowers and look like nobody else,
but this is the way they fought when Bacchus led them to war
and they beat the Sabaeans, rich from the incense trade, and the Arabs.
Bacchus broke through the frozen Hebrus' waters and left them
to get along however they could in those northern wastes,
but they're proud of their forebears' deeds that their strange regalia recalls.
Emoda's forces are there, and Exomatan soldiers assembled   150
beneath their proudly streaming banners. They're hunters and trappers
and famous breeders of horses — nobody's ponies are faster —
and they speed across the meadows and outrun lions and tigers,
and they'll grab a cub for a pet and leave the grief-stricken mother
far behind. The Toryni, too, have shown up, who live
by keeping honeybees, and the yellow-haired Satarchae,
who in peacetime are dairy farmers. The ardor for Phrixus' fleece
has also brought to Perses' encampment the skeptical Centors
and — as unlike them as one could imagine — the men of Choatrae,
whom people fear for their practice of black magic. They pray   160
in strange and violent rites to their terrible primitive gods
and can cast spells that are said to affect even the weather.
They can prevent the warmth of spring from bringing the trees
to leaf or can, if they choose, reverse the charm, and the frozen
surface of Lake Maeotis will suddenly thaw and wagons
that are making their way across will abruptly disappear.
The mightiest wizard among them, that master of Stygian practice,
Coastes, has come, but the clash of arms is not the attraction.
Instead, he hopes to see the one of whom he has heard
amazing reports — Medea, the maiden born in Cyta,   170
mistress of all those potent herbs that the region produces
and whose skill in the dark arts rivals even his own.
The shades of the Lake of Avernus are resting quiet, and Charon
is now untroubled: Coastes is not casting spells or communing
with those on the farther shore, and the moon can float undisturbed
on her course in a tranquil heaven, now that his incantations
are, for the time, suspended. And the Ballotini have come,

who are skilled in rapid maneuver. And the Moesian cavalry, too,
have joined the force — they are famous for changing from horse to horse
180 even at full gallop. The Sarmatians are there as well,
whose lances come with lines attached to their shafts — harpoons
they can use to deadly effect. It's amazing to see them all
together this way. Imagine Boreas driving the waves
that break on the shore, and he shouts in his piercing voice that his brothers,
the other winds, can blow as hard as they like but never
hope to match, with the serried assault of his powerful breakers.
The screams of eagles that fly over the mouths of rivers
are nothing compared to the blare of the trumpets that rise to heaven
from the plain where the frenzy spreads through the gathering host, as many
190 as leaves on the trees in the forest or flowers in springtime meadows.
The earth groans with the weight of the chariot wheels and quakes
at the rhythmic shocks of the men who are marching upon it in cadence.
One would think of the battering Jove hurled down from the heights
on Typhon on Phlegra's plain to beat him into the dust.

And opposing these, on the other side of the lines, Absyrtus
in his father's armor was chief, with the suitor Albanian prince
and the mighty kings with their thousands of mounted soldiers and footmen,
and among these, the son of Aeson stands forth with his band of heroes
and Pallas herself with her aegis that terrifies all who behold it —
200 alive with the Gorgon's snakes, eternally threatening fury
as much as they once did as a part of that monster's body.
They face that horde with Mars, with his lust for death, and the Fury,
Tisiphone, daughter of Night, who raises her head in the clouds
at the bugle's welcome sound, as Panic descends to earth
to stalk through the lines of battle and choose which hearts to enter.

And then? Then, steel met steel and shouts rang out, and heroes
felt the hot breath of heroes opposing and heard the clash
of metal striking metal, helm and shield and sword edge,
and the quieter sound of flesh giving way, and the cries of the wounded
210 and falling, and fallen, and broken bodies that squished underfoot.
There was carnage on every side, and empty helmets rolled
along the ground. There was body armor that filled with blood
that then drained into the dirt. There were sudden geysers of blood
as here and there the barbarians swarmed and shouted in triumph
or groaned in pain as their eyes closed to the daylight forever.

Caspius brought down Monaeses, one of Aeae's best,
dragged him off by the hair as the allied soldiers of Colchis
and Greece flung spears and stones, and then slashed the man's throat
and left the corpse on the field, disdaining to strip the armor,
but Aeëtes' forces, busied with other alarms and diversions,   220
could not retrieve the body. Caresus struck down Dipsas.
Strymon, from his place of concealment, used his slingshot
to pick off whomever he could, one man after another
—until Albanian Cremedon's sharp spearpoint hit home
and he fell and the wheels of the rushing chariots mashed him to pulp.

  Melas and Idasmenus advance toward one another,
and Melas throws his spear, but the light shaft wobbles and misses.
They close and fight hand to hand with their swords, and Melas hits,
and the other's neck is gashed by the blow, and he goes down.
It's madness out there, and bravery seems to count for nothing.   230
Ocheus falls, and Tyres, and neither one can guess
who did him in, and Iron just barely dodges the spear
of one of his own men when another some Pylian threw
comes in from the other side and hits, and he's down, and he's gone.

  Castor has seen the horsemen from the hills of Hyrcania charging
this way and that on impressive mounts that were bred for battle,
pure white and enormous, and it seems like a good idea—
irresistible, really—to get himself one of those horses,
so he runs out and plants his feet as Gela comes bearing down
and throws his lance and then jumps to avoid the horse, but the rider   240
is wounded and he keels over, and Castor pulls him down,
leaps up into the saddle, and grabs the reins himself,
and looking down from a cloud in heaven his father Jove
laughs in delight to see such a demonstration of grace.
Meanwhile, on the ground, the brother, Medores, is much less pleased.
In grief he rushes at Castor and prays to the gods above,
"Let me die too, or let my spear destroy this traitorous
horse that has failed to keep its rider safe and charges
now at me." But the words have hardly been pronounced
when an arrowhead that Phalerus has let fly punctuates   250
with its full stop—or ellipsis—his last sentence. He falls,
and his horse trots off to join its companion and stablemate.

  And Rhyndacus, have you come from Scythia's rugged mountains

and valleys to be undone by someone from Amyclae?
But Castor kills you and with you Tages, pierced in the groin,
the burly son of Taulas and a woodland nymph. He dies
despite all the care his mother and aunts put into his gear,
the gold-embroidered cloak, the yellow-feathered bonnet,
the brightly colored pants — and it's all ground into the dirt.
260 Now comes another horseman, a blur of energy, charging
this way and that through the fight wherever it's hottest, flinging
spear after spear and hacking to left and right with his sword,
which mows them down. To the aid of their falling companions, there comes
a band of savage Sarmatians, heavily armed and their ponies
also burdened with armor, and they set their lances and charge
with furious shrieks and they hurtle right through Aeëtes' lines
like so many huge machines. But they can't slow down or turn
as quickly as Castor who, riding with lighter equipment, can wheel
and circle around them. Enraged, they have no idea what to do.
270 The men from Colchis are also burdened down, and their chargers,
once committed, plunge forward to triumph or sometimes, as now,
to death — as Campesus falls from a spear between the ribs,
and he hits the ground and the shaft goes further and comes out behind.
Oebasus is down and he kneels and thinks that he's out of harm's way
but Phalces pokes a sharp lance in through his eye to the brain
and blood gushes down in a crimson flood from his cheek to his chest.
Near him is brave Sibotes, who trusts in his double-thick breastplate,
and he rises up to parry a blow from a mounted lancer.
He hits the point but its weight is too much for him to deflect
280 and it goes on into his body. Ambenus, now, with a spear
that has broken off in Sibotes' dying body goes on
and strikes with the shaft at Ocreus' trunk, and the shattered wood
wounds and kills. Now Taxes drags Hypanis along
half-dead and then altogether defunct, but Hypanis' spearpoint
is lodged in the ribs and Taxes yanks it and pulls the spear free,
but before the Scythian fighter can do much with it, Pollux
rushes upon him and kills him. His messmate, Oncheus, meanwhile,
is carried along by his horse on a headlong charge, and a pike
goes into his body. He tugs at the reins, but the horse keeps going
290 and the spear goes through and he feels the hot blood run down his back.

He thinks in that instant of fowling and how, when a bird is caught
in the clinging lime, he flaps his wings and tries to escape
but it's perfectly clear to the man and even the bird that it's over.
Panning right, we notice another encounter where Styrus,
Albania's prince and Medea's fiancé, meets Anausis,
who once had been her suitor. The former shouts out in delight
at this chance conjunction his proud defiance: "This is the man
whom King Aeëtes has picked to be his daughter's bridegroom.
But not so fast! It will never come to pass. The girl
I loved you shall never take to wife. And her meddling father,   300
like it or not, shall have his plans and his son-in-law
completely changed." Then, rushing forward, he hurls his spear
at the same time as the other. And Styrus is wounded and wheels,
yanking the reins of his horse and trying somehow to escape,
not having seen that Anausis is also stricken, is dying,
but still, from the ground he calls out with his last breath to his rival,
"Go on, run back to your witchy girlfriend, at home with her parents.
The wound I gave you is fatal, beyond her powers to cure
with her herbs and magic spells . . ." His voice is fading away
as the light fades from his eyes, and he feels a mortal chill   310
and a dizziness as his heavy head falls back on the ground.
      And now Gesander comes on, his spirit aroused by the battle's
frenzy of rage and grief, an intensification of life's
flavors, the bitter and sweet together. He chides his companions,
waving his naked sword over his head and calling
his fellow Iazyges slackers and trying to rouse their fervor
to something matching his own: "Our people's rigorous custom
is killing the old and feeble, but some, it seems, have escaped
and joined us here to dodder. Where is your pride? Your anger?
Let us advance together and attack the Argive positions   320
or else go home to our children and bid them cut our throats."
Saying this, he moves forward, invoking his father's ghost
to bless his efforts: "Dear and reverend father Voraptus,
give me the strength and courage to try to do you credit
so I may teach my children those lessons you once taught me."
In the world of shades his father hears his words and approves,
and Gesander, filled with his father's ardor, waves his sword.

On the other side of the line, Aquites, priest of the Phasis,
makes his way among the assembled troops with a vial
330   of that sacred river's potent water. He wears on his brow
and around his temples sprays of leaves of the poplar tree.
He is trying to find his son, Cyrnus, to keep him safe
and shield him somehow from the chances of war. He wanders here
and there on the field, calling out to his son, when a lance point whistles
beside his ear and Gesander's horse comes charging by
at full gallop. The priest turns and holds out his imploring
hands as he says, "For the white hair you see here on my head,
I ask for your father's sake that you spare my life, and, sir,
if you have a son, I ask that for his sake you spare mine."
340   But it does no good. Gesander thrusts home his scimitar
and says to the stricken priest, "My father is dead. I killed him,
for we prefer timely death to age and its shameful weakness.
If that son of yours felt love for you as well as his country,
he would have been here fighting, protecting you. To be young
and brave and strong is splendid. Die like a dog, unburied,
as you and your son deserve." The old man, expiring, prays
that the gods may yet keep his son from encountering such a savage.
        And now it is Canthus' turn, that Argonaut who had fetched
his arms from the ship that knew his fate and tried to warn him,
350   but couldn't. He takes his equipment, having reached the distant Phasis
and having survived to within a few days of beholding
that golden fleece they seek as a prize to bring home to Euboea . . .
He now meets Gesander, who, from his high horse, calls down defiance
to the man on foot: "Greek, you have traveled far, supposing
the entire world were nothing more than the farms and vines
you know in your native land, with its hillsides dotted with houses.
But this is harder country, colder, meaner, and we
are reared to a toughness that you can scarcely begin to imagine.
We don't go rowing with oars or trim our sails to the winds
360   to explore the world, which is not, in any event, a toy.
We ride on horseback on land or, in winter, on frozen water
across the wide steppes of Asia. We do not build city walls,
for we do not believe their illusions of safety and have no wealth,
no heaped-up pile of possessions we need to protect. Our worldly

goods we lug in a single wagon, which we can afford
to lose — as sooner or later everyone does. We value
freedom and live for the moment, happy to feast on our cattle
or the game we have found in the wilds. It's a lean, clean existence
your comfortable Argive peasants would find instructive, for life
is an endless battle and Mars' field extends as far   370
as the eye can see. On its hard ground with its icy streams
we rear our infant sons to the ways of flesh and carnage,
that they may survive in the endless and unremitting struggle
which is what we know life is." And driving home his point
he raises the shaft of his lance (its wood from some wind-whipped tree
in the furthest wastes of Asia's emptiness) and hurls it
into the breast of Canthus, where it passes through the rough
links of the bronze armor to his flesh, where the iron bites.
Idas and Meleager come running to try to help him,
and Amycus and Menoetius as well, but what can they do?   380
Telamon holds out his enormous shield to protect
his shipmate's corpse. Imagine in some defile a lion
protecting his cubs behind him from danger. So, steadfast,
does Telamon stand unmoving, Scythians now on all sides
of his seven-layered shield with which he can turn them away
even though they come back again and again in a swarm,
greedy for Canthus' arms that they're eager to strip from the corpse
on which they're no longer useful. But then, as the battle goes on,
that reason fades to an unimportant pretext that soon
is all but forgotten. They fight because they are fighting, a storm   390
of contesting winds and wills, as back in Aeolia's caves
the storms rage and the seas are whipped this way and then that.
Frenzy, a rage of the blood, drives them. The body is seized
and pulled one way and another, the way a bull's hide will get stretched
when the lord has turned the carcass over to servants to flense
and dress the skin with unguents and stretch it and turn it to leather.
That's what it's like with Canthus, whose body is pulled apart
and dragged in all directions, and neither side will let go.
Telamon holds at the waist and Gesander, furious, grips
the neck and the helmet's chin straps, but the helmet falls off and hits   400
the ground, making the noise of a hard-struck dinner gong.

He rushes again toward the body of Canthus, but Telamon's shield
is in his way, and the Minyae can drag their dead companion
back and manage to stow it in Euryale's car.
The Amazon whips her horses and speeds to attack, and the Greeks
follow along behind her and the rest of the Amazon band,
converging upon Gesander, who, seeing the women, exclaims:
"Are we to fight women, too? What shamelessness!" He throws
a spear and it strikes at Lyce beneath her breast, and another
410 hits Thoe just below the rim of her shield. He turns
at Harpe now, who is setting her bowstring and, near her, Menippe,
whose horse has stumbled and possibly lamed itself. He pauses,
deciding how to proceed and against which one, when the princess
Euryale comes up from behind him and strikes a blow
with her battle-axe with its heavy knobs of gold, and another
that splits his leather helmet and scalp and skull. He is staggered
as missiles hail down upon him. He holds his shield overhead
and lurches this way and that. Idas, whom nothing daunts,
feels fear as he watches him fall like a cliff giving way or a wall
420 where the mortar has slowly been washing away and its sudden collapse
brings catastrophe down on the mighty city that built it.
    And now comes Ariasmenus, feeling within his bones
the call of the moment. He charges, riding his car with the axles
from which sharp blades protrude that harvest horses and men,
and he bears down on the Greeks and the forces defending Colchis.
·Everywhere utter and absolute ruin . . . Think of the flood
when Jove sent down from Olympus that terrible deluge to drown
the world in Deucalion's time and Pyrrha's, and Alps were submerged
so that only their peaks protruded to break the surface as islands.
430 Such is the flood of destruction in Ariasmenus' wake
as he and his men hurtle across the field and back.
Then did Athena decide to show herself and her aegis
with Medusa's twining serpents, the heads of three hundred vipers
writhing and coiling, not to the men but to horses, which terror
seized at once, and they reared and flung back their helpless drivers,
and those cars with their cruelly slashing axles dealt out destruction
among their own and confusion and, following on that, panic.
Think of what happened in Rome when Tisiphone in her rage
brought in uncivil civil war two opposing legions

above whose lines on either side of the battlefield 440
were the same standards displaying identical warlike eagles.
The fathers of both had been friends and neighbors and plowed adjacent
fields that the Tiber watered, and the same levies recruited
their sons who now opposed one another. And so were these
companions whom fate divided, united only in fury
and the dealing of all but indiscriminate death in the panic
that governed the field as Pallas sped their runaway horses.
It's dreadful, with corpses piled up like sea wrack after a ship
has sunk and the waves deposit the mariners' broken bodies
on Libyan beaches along with the shattered hulls of their vessels. 450
There are corpses of men and of horses and pieces of corpses and entrails
those axles have mangled and dragged, dripping their trails of gore.
Aeëtes' forces, who cannot afford to indulge in pity,
continue to hurl their spears and shoot their arrows to slaughter
those who are wounded or trapped but still moving and groaning
in their last desperate moments. Hunters, sometimes, who pursue
their quarry with hounds or nets or those beaters' lines bedecked
with feathers, will find a helpless stag with its antlers snared
in the branches. The hunter, who now is merely a butcher, persists
in his purpose and kills the beast, but it isn't at all pretty. 460
Ariasmenus gathers his weapons and jumps to the ground
to fight on foot, but on left and right the chariots cut him
with the curved blades on their axles and they slice him to pieces and chew
the various parts of his body into their works so that nothing
of his remains remains touching the ground of the battle.

Thus were the men of Cyta and Colchis as well as the Minyae
dealing death to the Scythian hordes whom they put to rout,
when Juno, the Queen of Heaven, conceived a further refinement
to the plan she had in mind. This victory, fine in itself,
she knew would not achieve the purpose of Jason's quest 470
or get him the fleece, for she knew that the angry and faithless king
had deadly plots in his mind. Therefore, she went to Vulcan,
whose bulls she could see in their meadow, grazing and breathing flames
in Tartarean gloom. These beasts are those that the king will order
Jason to yoke and then to sow the teeth of the dragon . . .
What could she do to help him meet this impending challenge?
Medea then came to her mind, that maiden, skillful and potent

in the casting of spells and the working of charms at the altars of gods.
With herbs and juices and prayers she could halt the stars in their courses
480   and make her grandsire Phoebus stop in his rounds in the sky
aghast. She could summon rivers out of their beds and transform
even the lay of the land as she roused nature from slumber.
She could, by her spells, make the old and doddering youngsters again
and grant them a span of years more than the Fates had allotted.
She was the envy even of Circe, the greatest of witches,
and Phrixus had held her in awe, recognizing her powers
in the black arts as greater than any he'd seen back home
where sorcerers gather their poisons in Thessaly's meadows to cause
the moon in the sky to foam or ghosts to rise up from the earth.
490   She was the one whom Juno chose as the Minyae's ally,
for she might counter the bulls and their fiery breath and the crop
of warriors sprouting up from the ground. She was utterly fearless
and had never been known to shrink from evils that she might encounter.
Formidable, truly, this maiden, but think of her moved by passion.
What on earth could she not accomplish then? So Juno
betook herself to Venus' flower-bedecked bower,
and, as she approached, that goddess, attended by pretty putti,
arose from the silken pillows piled high on her couch of dalliance.
Quietly, almost with diffidence, Juno addresses her, saying,
500   "My hopes now rest in your hands. All that I've tried to accomplish
is yours to enable or else deny. Grant me your help
and favor, for what I am saying you know is the gods' truth.
Ever since Hercules' exile, Jove has been in a foul
temper: he checks me at every turn and is scowling and gruff.
He never comes to my bedroom at night as he used to do.
That ardor is all but forgotten. Help me rekindle the flame,
and teach me a few of your naughty temptress' tricks or lend me
some of those frilly adornments of your armoire that work
to drive men into a frenzy in heaven as well as on earth."
510   Venus is not at all fooled, but she, too, has tried to destroy
the Colchian land and Apollo's detestable race and can see
exactly what Juno is trying to do. At once, she agrees
and gives the other without any further pleading that awesome
aphrodisiac charm, the girdle that radiates lust
at a fever-heat to incinerate all caution and faith and shred

of honor in males, and prompts, at whatever peril, to sin.
"Take it," she says, "and know that with it go all my powers
and those of my busy Cupids. I hope it fulfills your desires."

The happy Saturnian goddess accepts the potent device
and transports herself at once to appear in the private chamber   520
of the Colchian princess Medea, where she puts on for the moment
the shape, voice, and manner of Chalciope, her sister.
She tries and almost succeeds in dimming her dazzling aura,
that divine fire that shimmers whether or not she wills it,
and because of which Aeëtes' daughter at once awakes
in trembling and fear. She addresses the frightened princess, saying,
"Everyone but you seems to know that the Minyae have come,
those men who have braved the dangerous depths of the sea to join
our father's forces here. The rest of the household crowds
to watch from the walls in wonder those heroes in heavenly armor,   530
but you remain asleep in your chamber, alone and indifferent.
When in your life will you have such a chance again to see
such princes?" She does not wait for an answer but, taking her hand,
leads — almost drags — Medea out of her bed and away.
Medea can hardly be said to have had a choice: if she thought
what evils waited along the path on which these were her first
innocent steps, to change her course was beyond her power.
She followed her *soi-disant* sister along the palace hallway
and up the turrets to see the Greeks — and to seem like a flower
that blooms in the spring mud for a poignant moment and then   540
decays and rots. Her local goddess, Hecate, mourned
at this, her devotee's end that she could see now as beginning:
"You poor dear, you are leaving our woodlands and maidenly bands
to wander among the Greek strangers in distant cities
where they will not treat you well. But I shall remain your protector,
faithful and true. Your departure will not go unnoticed. A captive,
you shall be nevertheless feared by your lord, who may prove
false, but I'll be his teacher, correcting his misapprehensions
that you, my dear handmaiden, and I may be trifled with thus."
Did Medea hear? The words were all but drowned out in the shouting   550
of the men below and the trumpets' blare. On the walls, the women
looked down in fear like birds who have taken shelter on branches
of the high trees in distress at the wail of an oncoming storm.

What they see, looking down, is carnage, the troops of the Getae falling
among the Drangaean dead strewn over the field and the mangled
corpses of allies who came from Hiberia only to cower
as they lay half-dead among broken weapons and wounded horses
from whose tangled and bloodied tack they struggle in vain to escape
as their groans and piteous cries resound in antiphon. Elsewhere,
560 the Geloni, their allies, enjoying a brief and local success
and quite unaware that the battle is already lost, are cheering
and chanting their curious native anthems and victory odes.
     What exploits were there that day, and splendid deeds of the brave!
Tell, O Muse, how it was, and recall for us now that frenzy
of such as Absyrtus, whose shield shone bright as his grandsire's car,
and whose quivering spear and menacing helmet strike fear in his foes,
who can hardly bear to look full face at his blazing glory,
but they turn and run away and his spear hits their fleeing backs
and his lumbering stallion's hoofs trample the flesh of the wounded.
570 As splendid as he is his comrade Aron, whose brazen armor
gleams in the light and whose cloak is bright with primitive totems
worked in the fabric that bellies before him or streams in the wind
behind and over his horse's crupper. Think of the morning
star and how Venus delights as it heralds the breaking day.
Such is the exaltation that Aron's appearance occasions.
Close by are fierce Otaxes and Rambelus, Scythian fighters
who have had no small success in the field against Colchian soldiers,
and deplorable Armes is there, whose contemptible practice it is
to deck himself with the hide of beasts and wear on his head
580 the horns of a stag. In this fashion he frightens or anyway puzzles
those troopers upon whom he springs in surprise — but Aron has seen him
and calls out a challenge: "We are no simple cowherds you're fighting,
but men at arms. That insulting getup will do you no good
except perhaps at night in the sneak assault of a coward.
You are no god or monster as you pretend. I wager
my life against yours upon it. Let us contend in battle."
Saying this, he plants his foot and he hefts his spear
and flings it into the target. That shaggy hide falls open,
revealing a mere mortal whose wound is gushing blood.
590 Phrixus' sons, Aeëtes' grandsons, acquit themselves
with similar honor in battle, eager to show their mettle

to their Asian kinsmen and the Greek heroes who also are kin,
among whom Jason himself delights to see their reckless
displays of courage wherever the fight is hot and heavy.
"Let heaven prosper you," he cries out over the tumult,
proud to think that they share his own Aeolian blood.
"Whatever prize I may seek, to find you is no small reward.
Whatever pains these labors may cause us, you are our solace,
whatever else, good or bad, the Fates may have in store."
But then he is busy, assaulting Suetes and then the mighty   600
Ceramnus, whom he dispatches, whirling his heavy shield
from the one to the other to clip the former behind the knee
and at almost the same instant to slash the latter's breast.
Not far away from him, Argus brings down two of the mounted
Scythians, Phalces, who crashes heavily down to the ground
and then Zacorus. Argus, on foot, then turns to Amastris,
whose blood he lets flow, as he coughs up disgusting gobs of gore,
and holds his belly but cannot contain the guts that spill forth
as he clenches his teeth in a rictus of pain that then relaxes
as the anguish and rage of his moment of life at last subside.   610
Calais kills Barisas and the mercenary Ripheus,
who would join in whatever war was on offer, but this was his last.
And he dies regretting that now he won't have the chance to spend
anything he had been promised — the oxen and hundred horses,
and a life of wealth and ease, but the wealth and the life are gone.
The Scythian Peucon falls, pretty and flaxen haired,
and at just that moment his mother, far away in her deep
Maeotian cave, laments, and her wail echoes over the lake
where her youngster used to play but will not return to again
to fish or sail, or in winter, when the surface is frozen, hunt,   620
tracking the herds of deer that venture across the ice.
Eurytus chases Exomatae, who flees from the field, while Helix,
pierced by Nestor's spear, expires — and with him dies
the hope of his father's house, for its line is now extinguished,
and that debt of care and love that children owe to their parents
is never to be repaid. Daraps kills Latagus
and Zetes, the one with a spear that pierces his breast, and the other
running away, surprised as his chest in an instant sprouts
an iron point and blossoms with gushes of crimson blood.

630　　　From up on the wall, Medea, perched on her bench, looks down
　　　　at these various scenes of combat, picking out those princes
　　　　she knows and can recognize, but at Juno's prompting, she spots
　　　　the splendid stranger, Jason, whose actions she follows, gazing
　　　　with eager eyes as he runs this way and that, inflicting
　　　　pain and death on men and horses with showering spears.
　　　　Wherever she looks in the hope of spotting her brother's armor
　　　　or that of her fiancé, there is that Jason again,
　　　　glorious, riveting, awesome, and now and then looking up
　　　　as if he can feel on his skin the weight of her passionate gaze.
640　　She has already guessed, but still she asks of her sister,
　　　　"Who is that man I keep seeing, who ranges all over the field
　　　　again and again amazing in demonstrations of valor?
　　　　You know the one I mean." And cruel Juno replies,
　　　　pleased to know that she's taken the bait and is hooked, "That man?
　　　　It's Aeson's son whom you see there, Jason, the Minyae's noble
　　　　leader, who crossed the sea to recover the fleece of his kinsman
　　　　Phrixus, as is his right. You see how brave and strong
　　　　he shows himself: he is second to none in all of Greece
　　　　in honor and line as he shines and flashes among his companions,
650　　the Minyae and our own Colchian chieftains, astride his heaps
　　　　of enemy corpses. And soon he will leave our shores to return
　　　　to Thessaly's wealth and ease, that country Phrixus longed for
　　　　and always held dear in his heart. One wishes him godspeed!"
　　　　Then she fell silent, seeing that Medea was paying no heed,
　　　　for her eyes were fixed on the hero's exertions down on the field.
　　　　　But the goddess was not content with rousing Medea's passion.
　　　　To Jason now she turned her attention, fanning the flames
　　　　of courage within his breast and urging her favorite forward.
　　　　Inspired, he now appears to be almost godlike. His eyes
660　　blaze from beneath his helmet, and its bright plumes shake in the breeze
　　　　like a star in the sky that twinkles in baleful omen to Perses
　　　　and to you, too, O maid of Colchis—a serious sign
　　　　like a meteor shower in autumn that Jove sends to betoken
　　　　the fall of unjust kings. The son of Aeson and grandson
　　　　of Cretheus felt in his limbs an uncanny strength that he used
　　　　to dominate his foe as he reared up, huge as a mountain,
　　　　one of the Caucasus, grim with winter's ice and snow,

to howl in the wind and frighten the wheeling Bears in the sky.
He roves the field like a lion that preys upon fatted calves
and the taste of the hot blood of the first is an appetizer   670
whetting his thirst for more, for a frenzy of gore and carnage
in which he rages, wielding his bloodied spearpoint and sword edge
on him and then upon him, until the ranks are diminished
of those who might think to stand up against this force of nature.
The long-haired Hebrus he smites, and Prion, the Getic hero,
and Auchus' head and arms he hacks from the trunk to send it
rolling along the slope of the field like some bleeding log.

    Elsewhere, the son of Jove, Colaxes, had reached the end
of his fated span, and his father in heaven, in grief, complained
at the woe of the human condition: "My own dear son! Alas!   680
And with all my godly strength I can do nothing to save him
without giving great offense to my brother and sister gods.
Neptune is now in mourning for Amycus, his son,
and other gods whose sons have fallen or soon will fall
would resent any interference on my part now for my son.
If I deny the others, then I must deny myself
as well, and allow the day of destiny's claim upon him
and every hero." Saying this, he bestows as his gift the final
measure of honor upon the unfortunate mortal, his son,
and inspires in him in his ultimate hour a limitless courage.   690
Over the battlefield he flies like a raptor, dealing
countless deaths throughout the opposing host's formations.
Imagine a sudden storm that comes up in winter from nowhere
to dislodge enormous boulders and devastate woodlands and fields,
and its torrents come sluicing down from the mountains' heights to rage
and then, somehow, subside, its strength spent, as its waters
run off into gullies that spill into brooks to flow downstream
to empty into the sea. Such is the violent beginning
of the last and most glorious moments of Jupiter's son as he darts
this way and that, and he first slays the brave Hypetaon   700
and Gessithous too, and then Arines and, after him, Olbus.
Wounded by now, and on foot after his horse is killed,
he brings down with thrusts of his lance Apres and valiant Thydrus,
a.k.a. Phasiades, whom Caucasus had sired
on the banks of the River Phasis where his father's flocks were grazing,

and therefore the parents gave their child the river's name
as a surname, meaning that he was to serve the river god
who, in his turn, might protect and prosper their little boy.
In the manner of certain Eastern cults, they never allowed
710 that his hair be cut—but the parents' hopes prove to be vain,
and Colaxes brings him down. He turns now to other foes,
but Juno, the cruel goddess, breaks this string of his triumphs
as Jason now draws near. Defiant, Colaxes greets him
and asks, "Have you come this far to feed your corpses to Scythian
curs and carrion birds?" And he picks up a rock from the turf
the horses' hooves have churned, hefts it an instant, and flings it,
but Juno turns its path away from Jason's head
and it hits, instead, Monesus, unknown and unlamented,
and he falls down dead before he has hit the ground, but Aeson's
720 son's spear rides true through the air to pass through the other's
shield and strike his heart, and, dying, he looks up to see
the face of the murderous Jason blocking the fading sun.
Jason looks down for a brief moment, then hurries away
to harry the luckless Alani, who know him all too well.

From the top of the wall, the princess' bright eyes follow the hero
in whom the fire of Juno is raging hotter than ever,
but Medea's taste for the scene is less than it was. She is troubled
and turns to the sister beside her—and she feels a moment of doubt.
Is it really she? Is there something strange about this familiar
730 face? And has she the nerve, if it isn't her sister, to question
or challenge whatever person—or goddess—she could be?
Instead, she feels herself yielding once more to the lovely languor
and delicious fancies that shimmer in the tongues of her heart's flame.
We all know of those gentle southern breezes that tousle
the topmost boughs of trees and ruffle their leaves but turn
suddenly strong to buffet the helpless ships at sea.
This is the way it was with Medea in those first moments
that led her on to her fits of madness. She fingers the necklace
that flashes around her helpless neck, and its lustrous gold
740 seems to melt the strength of her limbs. She gives it back
to the goddess, not displeased by the gemstones or crafted metal
but afraid of the feelings of passionate wildness that rouse in her shreds
of maidenly shame while they rouge her cheek with delicate blushes.

She speaks: "Do you think, dear sister, that our father will keep his promise?
What perils that Argive stranger faces whom Providence brought us,
and all on behalf of strangers!" Before she has finished, Juno,
knowing now that she has accomplished her purpose, leaves,
but Medea does not think to follow her sister. More boldly
she leans out over the wall to watch as the warriors swarm
and beset the son of Aeson. Those arrows and spears his foes   750
are aiming at him she feels, and each one wounds and stings.
At the shaft from Lexanor's bow she cringes and ducks, and it misses
Jason, goes over his head, and finds its target in Caicus.
Poor man! You leave behind you a wretched wife, a bride,
bereft now of her bridegroom, whose sudden loss she mourns.
     Myraces had come to Aeëtes' aid, a Parthian
diplomat, to sign a treaty of friendship, but fate
and the outbreak of fighting had trapped him, and he and his pretty eunuch
squire had joined in the battle to fight with their Colchian allies.
He holds the elaborate reins of his Eastern chariot hung   760
with richly embroidered cloths. He wheels and charges to speed
toward where the fighting is hottest. On his head he wears a tiara
bejeweled with bright green stones embedded in silken inserts.
With his arms bangled with gold, he brandishes the blade
of his scimitar that glints in the sunlight. His Eastern trousers
are tucked in his boots. The outfit catches the Scythian eye
of the fierce Syenes, who flings his spear at the tiger-head
shield, and it pierces the face of the beast, and the blood of its owner
gushes forth from the mouth of the emblem to spill on the ground.
The eunuch, meanwhile, has fallen, and his crimson cloak is stained   770
with the red of his blood, which also colors his face and hair
that his mother had decked with gold and perfumed with rich Sabaean
flowers' attar. Picture an olive tree one has tended
with constant toil and care in the hope of its yield of fruit,
but a hurricane's winds come swooping out of the north to uproot it,
and all that remains is its wreck stretched out on the wounded earth.
Such was Miraces' fall that Medea watched in dismay
but relief, too, for the other, for whom she cared, had been spared.
What were Talaus' trials to her, or the furious charges
of brave Meleager, or even the perilous exploits she saw   780
of Acastus? Yet each of them risked a life that was dear to his kin.

And the men on the field were all well aware as the battle raged
that the tide of events had declared itself as the flow of blood
of the fallen soaked into the ground and the troops of the bested
forces withdrew, or their chariots rattled, aimless and empty,
where once their mighty lords and chieftains had stood so proud.
    Perses, ignoring the cries of his routed and fleeing companions,
looked up to the heavens to cry in protest: "You gods up above,
why did you mislead me? Why did you give me omens
790 that lured me from home to stir up my Scythian forces and set
this altogether misguided battle in progress? Your augurs
lied! You promised me, Jupiter, triumph over my brother.
You let me believe these Argive strangers would join in my cause.
To live in the light is to learn to endure such gross betrayals.
What man of honor can bear it? Better to die! And yet
I ask that the Fates may grant me one more day—to betray
the Achaeans and bring them to ruin also, as they have deserved.
Let me live to behold Jason, so proud of his prowess,
cheated and hating his efforts when all will have come to nothing."
800 Thus he spoke, and he groaned and he beat his armored breast
and wept copious tears, enough to have filled his helmet.
And yet he advanced to fight, to the enemy's strongest point,
to kill or else be killed, but Pallas saw him and thought,
"Perses is throwing away his life, but my father's decree
is that he should one day rule in his brother's place over Colchis.
I cannot risk provoking my father's severe chastisement
by letting him die." So saying, she shrouded him over with mist
and intervened to prevent those javelins flung by the foe
and hissing about him from even touching a hair of his head.
810 A sudden wind comes up to pluck him out of the fray,
waft him through shimmering air, and set him down somewhere
at the far edge of the field, distant from any fighting,
where Hiberian troops and those of the Issedonians, held
in reserve, contributed nothing but shouts and cheering words.
    And now Night brings on the shadows men have longed for, and stars
shine serene and silent as the noise of the combat is lulled.
The girl on the walls, exhausted from her daylong ordeal of terror,
comes down at last. The Nyctelii, those devotees of Bacchus,
at the start of their pious revels, resist the god for a time

but then give in to their frenzy. In such a state does Medea
return and feel herself yielding, as she sees with the Colchian troops
the Greek fighters and there, among them, the splendid Jason
for whom she feels such longing, an all but unquenchable passion
to gaze at him in his armor, his body, his noble face.

Book VII

Night comes on, that time that ought to bring lovers together
in sweetness and joy, but you, Medea, must go to your bed
alone, heartsick with longing for that man who has come to Colchis
from Thessaly's far-off shores. In the dark, she lies down restless,
unable to sleep, and not even knowing what stirs her so.
She can hardly think, cannot admit to herself the obsession
that holds her in rough embrace. Her mind is a giddying whirl
of scenes of the day and the battle and images of that face,
and she tries to talk herself out of this passion that feels like a sickness:
10 "How stupid this is! What madness or folly, that I am possessed
by thoughts of that man that I cannot put out of my mind, a stranger
from across the ocean's endless expanse! What have you done?
What have I let you do? I used to be able to sleep
like a normal person. If only he'd take that fleece of his kinsman
and be on his way. That sheepskin of Phrixus is all he wants.
He hasn't come here for me. And soon he'll be gone forever.
He'll never come back, nor will we visit Haemonia's cities . . .
Like it or not, I have to learn to face this truth—
that I'll never see him again." And then she thinks of his shipmates
20 and burns with envy that they who came with him here will leave
and follow their valiant leader home, while she remains
behind, bereft. She wishes he'd go so that she could begin
the painful process of grieving. She tosses and turns in her bed,
unable to find any comfort or ease in any position.
At last, the room resumes its shape, and she sees in the doorway
the light of the coming day as the morning star shimmers

and fades away as she hopes that her torment also may fade,
and she rises renewed as the ears of wheat in the field are refreshed
by an early-morning shower, or, better, say, spent oarsmen
whose strength is renewed as they feel a morning breeze on their backs.   30
The Minyae, meanwhile, are scheming, planning their next step
in fulfilling their journey's purpose. They go to meet with the king,
and Jason, respectful, is patient as they wait for the monarch to finish
reciting his prayers of thanks and offer his trophies of war
to the tongues of flame that blaze on the gods' hungry altars.
As they wait the crew are casting their glances this way and that
and they hope, perhaps, to catch in the royal hall or the courtyard
some golden glint of the sacred pelt for which they have come.
    Jason is still composing himself, preparing to speak
and putting on a confident but not too friendly smile,   40
when the king preempts him, seizing the moment and pouring forth
that venomous anger he has until now had to conceal:
"Sons of another world, aliens coming here
from the end of the earth where you may or may not belong, what madness
has driven you here? Is it friendship you feel in your hearts for me?
Phrixus came to bring me only grief! I wish
he had drowned in the sea with his sister, and that I'd never heard his name
or the names of any Greeks. Who is this Pelias, king
of Thessaly? Where is that? What business is it you strangers
can have with me? The Cyanean rocks should have kept you away.   50
A boat with fifty outcasts and desperadoes lands,
and I, a sovereign ruler, am to give you whatever you ask,
yielding, without a fight, what is part of my national treasure?
To robbers and pirates? You think we Asians are less than human,
and that you can just come and take what you want? Our precious gold?
Why not our daughters, too? Where you come from, do you have parents?
Families? Homes, perhaps? Or are you a band of brigands,
savages roaming the earth, who live on what you can plunder?
Outlaws, I shouldn't wonder, and exiles your angry king
has forbidden to come home ever — except with that fleece, a bribe   60
he might accept. But before I give that up, those mountains
will come down here with their forests felled to dance on the shore
and swim in the sea like dolphins in the wake of your Greek ship.
Before I give you the fleece, Helle, whose image is here

decked with funereal chaplets, shall swim to the surface and breathe
and laugh out loud for joy! You had better begone unless
you are magicians whose ship has strange and mystical powers
to cloud men's minds . . . I'll make you an offer—take it or leave it.
You want the fleece? It's yours, if first you will go to the Plain
70   of Mars outside the city's walls. It's a wasteland now
after many years of neglect, but the bulls are there to be yoked,
as I once could do, but not anymore. They do not know me,
don't recognize me now, and are almost wild again:
flames shoot out of their nostrils and gaping stertorous mouths.
Prove your valor, stranger, harness those bulls, and plow
that field again and plant the seed I used to sow there.
I could do it once, and if you can do it, the fleece
is yours. Consider my offer. If your wooden vessel has power,
let it help you now undertake this farmer's labor
80   I ask of you—and burn to death, as I hope you will do,
in the breath of those terrible bulls. Or would I prefer to see you
survive that trial to die as the well-armed soldiers spring up
from the earth's furrows you've plowed, as seeds of the serpent of Cadmus
sprout and blossom to yield their rich harvest of death?"
        His daughter marveled, hearing his puzzling words that soon
unfolded in her mind, and her face turned pale as she looked
across the room to Jason and was gripped by fear for his sake.
She trembled to think how, brave as she knew he was, he might choose
to take that impossible dare, imagine he might be equal
90   to this inhuman task, try his chances, and lose
as any mortal would. Jason, too, was dumbstruck
in anger more than dismay, for this was not what they'd bargained.
Imagine some trading vessel: the weary captain, at last
spying that longed-for lighthouse that stands at the Tiber's mouth,
sets his helmsman's course but discovers, instead of home port,
that he's suddenly back in the shoals of Syrtes off Carthage's coast.
Astounded, thus, is Jason and he tries to think what answer
to make to this lawless and impious ruler. At length he rises
and, with some restraint, declares: "This is not what we agreed.
100   When we put on our armor, Aeëtes, to help you fight off the rebels,
this is not how you were speaking to the Minyae you needed then.
What do your promises mean? In guile you are Pelias' match!

Do you perhaps conspire together against me? The ocean
is crossed, but you conjure up another ocean of troubles.
But I won't be stopped! O tyrants, come, vent your hatred upon me.
With the strength of my head and heart, so familiar with trials and hardship,
I defy you, each and all. I beg of you only one favor—
that if I do not survive, and this harvest of men with spears
vanquishes me, or I'm killed in the flames of those bulls' mouths,
send to Pelias' cruel ears that I and my comrades   110
died here while attempting to follow his outrageous orders,
and ask, if he can find some person he trusts, that my body
be brought back home to repose in the earth of my native land."
      He turned and strode from the chamber, leaving the king astonished
and his daughter devastated. She could barely contain herself
as she gazed at his back, those broad shoulders, that neck, and then
at the gate, that empty space through which he had passed. She felt
the very soul within her straining as if on a tether,
eager to follow. She wished that the room and the palace could move,
stirred by her ardor to follow and walk the paths he had trod.   120
She thinks of Io, who stood at the shoreline, now stepping forward
and now, in her fear, retreating, as the Erinys drive her onward,
and she knows how that must have felt to be tugged both ways at once.
She paces the room and passes the window through which she peers,
and then she looks to her father and tries without speaking to will him
to change his mood and mind and summon the Minyae back.
Distracted, she wanders from room to room till she falls exhausted
upon her lonely bed, which she flees to go to her sister.
She wants to confide, to tell Chalciope what's in her heart,
but cannot, or dare not. The words refuse to form in her mouth.   130
She leaves. She returns and asks her sister to speak of Phrixus
and how he came from a distant land to settle in Colchis,
or perhaps to talk of Circe, their aunt, and how she was carried
wonderfully once through the air by a team of wingèd serpents.
But even for this, her favorite story, she has no patience,
and wanders away to seek among her handmaidens solace
and comfort. She goes to her parents and clings to them like a child.
She takes her father's hand in her own and gives it kisses.
She is like some cosseted dog that has lived its life on cushions
or else in its mistress' lap, and has nibbled on table scraps   140

but now is stricken, distempered, and runs from room to room
with its eyes rolling in madness and whimpering in its distress.
Angry at what she now has allowed herself to become,
she blames herself for her madness, admits she is being a fool
to torture herself with his image that she summons up before her,
and tells herself that his ship has already sailed; he has fled;
and before he reaches home he surely will have forgotten
even her name. "Who is he that I should care so much?
What does it mean to me if he fails in his quest and Greece
150 grieves and is shamed?" But she wishes nevertheless that his death
could be elsewhere. She prays that the god grant that favor.
He is kin, after all, to Phrixus, who married her own dear sister.
She recalls, on his behalf, his account of how he was sent
by the harsh command of his king to sail the seas, and she wishes
that all may be well and that he may survive, and not hate her father,
although she has no clear notion of how that could come about.
She throws her weary body upon her bed in the hope
of sleep's release, but vivid dreams assail her cruelly,
with Jason kneeling, imploring her father, the king, who refuses
160 whatever he asks. She startles and wakes, and it takes her a moment
to recognize her maidens in waiting, who gather about her
and the home she knows and loves. Estranged, she felt like a stranger
wandering somewhere through towns of distant Thessaly, exiled
as was Orestes, they say, who, driven by Furies, roamed
the earth, an outcast, blinded by hatred and fear, and seized
a sword with which to slash and stab his mother's guards.
The Furies' vipers bit and stung and they lashed his back
as he tracked his mother down, that whore who murdered his father.
Dreaming each night of wreaking upon her that vengeance her crime
170 required, he woke each morning and had to begin again
for justice's sake, and his own, and that of his sorrowing sister.

    Juno looks down, distressed that the Colchian princess wavers,
her reason struggling still against the force of her passion.
It's no good now to assume the sister Chalciope's likeness.
She requires some stronger measures or else must face the shame
of having her will defied by a woman, a mere mortal.
She rises up to float through the thinness of air and seeks out
Venus high on Olympus' numinous peak. This goddess

Juno addresses: "For your help thus far, I give you my thanks,
but the girl is obdurate still and in anger struggles against me.   180
I am losing her. I therefore implore you, go to her now
yourself and extort from her that victory I require.
Embolden her heart to a wanton madness that she may dare
to leave her father's house and defend with all her wiles
my noble hero, Jason, and keep him from all misfortune.
And that serpent that guards the grove where the golden fleece he seeks
hangs . . . Let her enchant it with the potions of her black arts,
lure it down from its ash tree, and put it deeply to sleep.
You do your part in this: the rest of the undertaking,
I give to the care of the Furies and the young maiden herself."   190
        The mother of all those wingèd Cupids answered the Queen
of the Gods, saying, "I did not fail to help you before,
when first you asked me to bend and melt that maiden's heart
and initiate her to a kind of trouble she'd never imagined.
I gave you that charmed sash that had its effect — it shook her
and almost forced her to yield. But I see that her wavering spirit
seems to require my own attention and strenuous effort.
But I will have my way and she shall pine and tremble
with longing she cannot endure for union with that Greek chieftain.
Let him go at once to visit Diana's shrine, where the maidens   200
of Colchis dance their rites and pray to the triple goddess,
waving their sacred torches. Hecate's dismal powers
are nothing for us to fear: let her appear or attempt
to interfere with our purpose, and even she will feel pangs
of passion stir for the *Argo*'s captain to whom we give aid,
and she will come herself to subdue those monstrous bulls
in the hope of a grateful embrace." Hearing this, Juno dispatches
wingèd Iris and bids her carry out Venus' command
and see that the son of Aeson appears in that holy grove.
Iris looks for the Minyae, while the goddess of Cytherea,   210
Venus, finds the maiden, and Juno settles back ·
on the heights of the Caucasus' crags to watch with her hopes high
Aeaea's walls below and see how events unfold.
        Venus has hardly emerged from hiding into the city
when in the maiden's heart she introduces new sickness,
a turmoil redoubled from what she felt before, a deeper

longing, a more abysmal grief. She fills Medea's
mind with attractive fancies and lets her compose in her head
elaborate speeches with which she might address the hero:

220 "If only your mother were here to help you with secret spells
the women in Greece must know . . . Your mother or even your wife?
(Do you have a wife at home?) What can a young girl do,
seeing you in this plight, but grieve at your dismal prospects?
Oh, how I hope to be spared having to see your mangled
corpse brought back to the court — I would have to join my sister
in a life of mourning. I wonder, can Jason suspect what I'm thinking?
He supposes he is alone, that no one cares for his fate,
that none fears for his peril, and that none would grieve his loss
or even remember his name. He thinks, not without reason,

230 that every face he encounters here in this alien land
is indifferent or hostile, and he, in turn, must hate us all
without exception. And yet, those ashes of his, and the bones,
whatever is left from the ravaging bulls' consuming fires,
I shall tend with honor and give them a sanctified resting place
so that I may at last declare to his ghost at his tomb my love."

These words of hers were scarcely ended when there, on her bed,
the goddess Venus appeared in the shape of the lovely Circe,
Titan's daughter, Aeëtes' sister, and aunt to Medea,
wearing her sacred robe with its occult signs and symbols

240 worked in the fabric, and wielding her famous magic wand.
Medea thinks at first she is still dreaming, but slowly
comes to understand that she is awake and this
is no mere figment but really her aunt who has come to her aid,
and in joy she welcomes the goddess with tears and many kisses,
addressing her: "O Circe, you have come back to your own
land and people, and at just the time when I most need you.
Did your team of marvelous serpents carry you here? From where?
What land, what place in the world could there be as pleasing as this,
my father's kingdom? Jason has come with a ship, braving

250 the ocean's perils. And did this somehow remind your heart
of its love of your native country?" She would have gone on, but Venus
interrupted and answered, "You are the cause of my visit.
You are no longer a child. You must know that the world is rich
in heaven's gifts, which are shared and spread all about the earth

and among mankind, on whom the gods look down as they
in turn look up to the skies. Wherever the sun shines
in its daily course, we may learn rightly to call our own.
Do not upbraid me, then, for leaving this frigid climate
and seeking elsewhere a milder and easier kind of life
that I enjoy with my consort Picus, Latium's king.   260
The meadows there are not troubled by flame-snorting bulls, and over
a most pacific and gentle Tuscan sea I delight
to preside and even preen. And you, what suitors are here
among whom you may choose? Some Sauromatian yokel,
Hiberian savage, or fierce and crude Gelonian tribesman
to whom you would be one of the many wives in the household?
The thought of it makes me shudder!" When the goddess fell silent, Medea
replied straightaway, correcting, if not contradicting, her aunt:
"I am not without resources, but as one of Hecate's adepts,
I have, as you may imagine, spells, potions, and charms   270
and will not be driven away to my fate like a tame heifer.
Do not be concerned for me — or anyway not for that reason.
I have other, more pressing troubles for which I require help
that you may be able to give. I am wretched, tormented in spirit,
troubled in mind, and even afflicted in body — my mouth
is dry. I cannot sleep at night. At least in that
you may provide some cure with your powerful wand with which
you may touch my troubled eyelids. O aunt, I turn to you now
as a daughter might turn to a mother, in pain, perturbed, perplexed.
You cannot appear this way, give me reason to hope,   280
and then not help me. That would be cruel, and I should be desperate.
I am engaged to be married to a man for whom I feel nothing,
and everything conspires against me, even you,
my aunt, whom I love . . . You could be a Gorgon with snakes in your hair!"
And there she broke off, collapsing in Venus' arms and weeping
with shuddering sobs that racked her body as if she had plague
that made her heart and brow burn with its killing fever.

       Venus holds the girl in her tender but baneful embrace,
and kisses her with fateful kisses, sweet as their poison,
inspiring love, which has as its darker aspect frenzy.   290
"There, there," she says, as she comforts her sobbing niece, "lift up
your face, poor dear. Listen, I'll tell you a curious tale

of something I saw as I landed after my trip through the air
from my home in the West. I saw in the harbor here a ship,
a splendid vessel whose like may one day come to my island.
Its crew were handsome fellows, but their leader, their captain and prince,
was the best-looking of all. And thinking that I might know you,
might be your companion at court, he approached and spoke to me, thus:
'Lady, as one who is fated soon to die, I beg you,
300   if you feel any compassion for one in my sorry plight,
exposed as I am to horrors beyond description, do me
a service and take this word to the ear of your young mistress.
Speak to her of my sorrows and say I pray to her image
I keep in my mind and I hold out my suppliant hands to her
as I do to Minerva and Juno, those goddesses who brought me
hither and kept me alive and unharmed through a thousand perils.
But they appear to have failed me, and now I turn to her,
my last remaining hope, if only she hears my prayer
that she lend her aid to me and these lives that are in my charge.
310   Let her at least remember our names and who we were—
an act of perfect kindness I can never hope to repay,
unless I am saved from a cruel death, in which event
I am hers, body and soul. Will she have pity upon us? . . .'
And here he broke off and drew his sword, as if he would fall
on the naked blade and end at once his desperate existence.
But I stopped his hand and promised. I beg you, do not fail him.
I was moved by this hero's words and prompted to help him myself,
but I report his request to you to whom he addressed it.
I have accomplished enough and established my name and fame,
320   and I offer you this chance for the glory of which you are worthy.
Think how Hippodamia's help to her suitor Pelops
earned her great renown, or consider Ariadne
without whom Theseus never could have succeeded in Crete.
This is your life's great moment, to which the before and after
will forever refer. Can you not give help to this noble stranger?
Let death come instead to that harvest of Cadmus' serpent's teeth
and put out at last those flames of your father's fearsome bulls."

     During much of this speech Medea's eyes had been rolling wildly,
showing the whites as those of a spooked horse will do, and her hands
330   fluttered like angry birds as if to strike at the face

of the goddess whose words had stirred such a tumult of shame within her,
and now the wretched maiden covered her ears with her pillow
to silence that all but unendurable voice, and her limbs
shuddered as if with ague. She thought to run but could not
make herself move, or even imagine which way to go,
and she longed for the grave's sweet silence and the weight of the mute earth,
from which, if they could but feel it, corpses could take great comfort
and at whatever cost put an end to this spate of battering words.

   The goddess commands her to follow and waits at the gate for the girl,
who moves as though in a dream to do as she has been bidden.   340
One thinks, perhaps, of Pentheus, putting on the raiment
from his mother's closet, the bacchant's gown and the other regalia,
the spear and timbrel, to go and invade those forbidden precincts
of the god with the wine-stained headdress — and there be done to death.
Medea looks about her and is struck by the thought: this room
she has lived in and takes for granted, is she leaving it now forever?
Her footsteps drag, but she cannot resist the double pull
of her passion and Jason's danger. The words she has heard still burn
in her ears and her soul, and what can she do? She knows full well
that she is about to betray her country, her king and father.   350
She can see the infamy coming her monstrous crimes will earn
and she wearies the gods above and below with her cries of protest
that this is not what she wants or in any way has deserved.
She falls on the ground and flails with her fists as if to knock
at the doors of death and ask the Queen of the Underworld
to grant her the gift of death — to admit her at once and fetch
that man as well to her realm of shadows, the cause of her madness.
Pelias she blames, who dispatched on this ruinous errand the blameless
hero — for whom she feels again a rush of compassion,
and she thinks of how with her skill she can bring him through his trials.   360
But she cannot, ought not, must not. Better that she should die,
or they both should die together, than that she should yield to this base
and baseless love, for a stranger to whom she owes nothing at all.
She gets up; she lies down on her bed; but she feels again that summons
she cannot ignore and she thinks she hears the heavy grating
the hinges make on the gates of the palace swinging wide.

   Utterly vanquished, shameless, beyond any sense of shame,
in thrall to a strange power beyond her strength to fight,

she goes to her cabinet now to find those charms and potions
370   strong enough to be useful for the Greek captain's purpose.
The obedient doors, on their own and without her touch, fly open
and she looks at the strange collection, gleaned from the ocean's floor
or the land of shades, or collected at night when the moon was red,
and she thinks to herself that here is the help she needs — to avoid
betraying her father and country: she can bring her life to an end
with any one of these potent poisons she has at hand.
That bitter death she can have with a quick gulp, she deserves
for giving in as she has to the stupid promptings of love.
But she cannot bring herself to turn away from the sweetness
380   of life and light and even of love. She shakes her head
and cries aloud, "Alas!" For the death of a girl in the prime
of youth? For her loss of the man who never became her lover?
She thinks of her dear brother Absyrtus. Will she never see
the down come onto his boyish cheeks as he grows toward manhood?
If she kills herself, she imagines how deeply her brother will grieve,
and from this she tries to summon a degree of anger toward Jason . . .
Why did her father bid him even that guileful welcome,
rather than kill him outright? That would have been better by far
for everyone concerned and, most of all, herself.
390   She can neither take her life nor even take charge of it; rather,
she will submit and resign herself: she will act at Circe's
direction. "Ah, Circe, daughter of Titan, I yield
and rely on your wisdom; I trust in you and hope you may lead me
aright." Having said this, she thinks again of the young Greek
and gives herself over to feelings of pity and worry. Ready
to brave either love or death, for his sake, she offers a prayer
to Hecate to send her greater powers that she can use
on his behalf and stronger potions and drugs. What she has
she takes, including her best, an herb from the Caucasus' wilds
400   of enormous power that sprang from blood Prometheus spilled
as the bird was gnawing his liver, and the blood splashed from its beak
to drop on the grass where snows and icy winds and hoarfrost
gave its exotic flower a preternatural toughness
such that it can withstand even bolts of lightning
that cannot blemish its verdant leaves. Hecate herself
could cut through its toughened stem only by using a blade

tempered in Stygian springs, and she showed her handmaid the blossom.
Medea then by moonlight in the tenth month used to gather
from the grim heights of the mountain specimens for her charms
against mortality, each of them touched with the blood of the god   410
who looked down in his anguish at the princess from Colchis and groaned
as she wielded her sharp sickle and his fettered body was racked
with spasms of fresh pain as the blade cut through the stalks.
　　With this and other such nostrums that to her own people
and kingdom are deadly poison the young girl equips herself
and she feels how her limbs tremble as she ventures into the night
where Venus takes her hand and offers her comforting words
to soothe her terrors and leads her through the city's darkened streets.
Imagine a nervous bird who nudges out of the nest
her frightened fledglings to launch them out into thin air   420
to fly on their still weak wings, and she feels their shudders of fear
and hears them implore that they might return to their nest and the safety
of the topmost branch of their tree: so does Medea tremble
as she passes by the familiar walls of the city's silent
houses on streets she has always known that are suddenly strange.
Again, as she did at her own threshold, she hesitates,
and tears well up in her eyes as the passion burns in her breast.
She asks the goddess beside her: "Is it true? Does Jason himself
ask for me? Did he speak my name? Am I doing right?
Am I not being immodest or forward or even mad?   430
Ought I not feel some shame? And does he not mind begging
for a girl's help?" The other made no reply, but stopped
her dithering words and nudged her along the road to the shrine,
where they heard in the darkness the eerie sounds of incantations
and magic spells that made the wood sprites hide their faces,
while the rivers shrank in their beds and the mountains seemed to turn
their shoulders away in unease. In the stalls of the barns was terror
and out in the sheepfolds, alarm. Even the graveyards stirred
with deathly panic, and Night itself was gripped with fear.
Venus, leading the way, quailed but tried to appear   440
unruffled as she led the girl to the triple goddess'
tree-shaded shrine. Abruptly, from out of the shadows, Jason
appeared and startled them both, the fearful princess first,
who was unaware how, on one side, Iris rose through the air

while, on the other, Venus let go the hand she'd been holding.
Imagine, on some pitch-black night, the frozen panic
that can seize the shepherd as well as his flock . . . Or, better yet, think
of that terrified anguish the sightless and voiceless ghosts must feel
when they bump into one another in the deepest abysses of hell,
450 and extrapolate from that what these two felt in the grove
when they came together there in the spooky murk of midnight.
Sometimes at night when a storm comes up you can see the trees,
the slender cypress or fir, tremble in what resembles
fear, and the wind whips up, and they reach out to one another
with their topmost branches to touch as if they tried to exchange
what comfort and reassurance their woody hearts can feel.
    Anyway, there they were, face to face, not moving,
not saying a word, each hoping the other would speak. Medea
longs for Jason at least to raise his eyes and look
460 into her eyes and say her name, and Jason sees her,
dumbstruck, weeping, lovelorn, blushing with shame, and he speaks:
"Do you bring me some glimmer of hope, a light in this utter blackness?
Is it pity that brings you here to see my labors? Or scorn?
Do you come here simply for entertainment, to watch me die,
taking the cruel delight you have learned, perhaps, from your father?
But how can so lovely a face mask such a savage heart?
I cannot hope to fathom such people as these whose thanks
for the service we have done them is abrupt and total betrayal.
You heard what your father said and witnessed what happened. I ask you,
470 was it right? Was it fair for a man to behave that way? Your father
would have me battle with monsters! Was it for this that Canthus
gave his life on the field to an enemy spear or Iphis,
our dear friend and shipmate, died for your city's sake?
For all those Scythian fighters we slew, your enemies, this
is how we should be rewarded? Your father, had he been honest,
could simply have told us to leave his realm, but he gave me hope
and you see with what double-dealing he makes his promises good.
To be able and even willing to die is within my power,
which is all one needs to maintain one's honor. I will not refuse
480 to undertake what your father commands me to do, as I will not
consider leaving without that fleece for which I was sent.
Do not think to see me give up, turn tail, and run."

Thus he spoke and she, now that he'd fallen silent,
tried to reply, but could not produce the words she wanted.
How could she order her feelings and thoughts, much less the language
with which to express that tumult that roiled within her, the fear
that mixed with her love and shame? How to begin? And how
to proceed from there? At length she lifts her eyes to meet his
and forces herself to speak: "Why did you come to this land
from Thessaly, far away? And what do you want from me?   490
Without my help those labors you undertake for my father
are hopeless, as you must know. Had I given in to my fears
and had I not left my father's palace to come to your aid,
you would be facing a certain and horrible death—and I
should also perish from grief. Where is your patroness, Juno? Where
is her sister goddess, Minerva, now that you need her most?
Who is here to help you but a native princess, a stranger
from whom you have no right to expect any show of kindness
in the time of your misfortune? Do you know how lucky you are?
This woodland that thinks it knows me and sees what I'm doing wonders   500
if this is Aeëtes' daughter. I am strange to myself as my fate
is overwhelmed by yours. But take these gifts I bring you,
but if ever Pelias sends you on another impossible mission,
do not expect that your beauty will save you a second time."
She was still speaking but had already reached into her bosom
to draw forth the magic herbs she had brought and the potent charms
that she clutched tight. "But wait," she said. "If those gods you trust
can bring you through this ordeal in safety, alive and well,
or if your own strength is enough and you don't need help from me,
then send me away, I beg you, and let me go home to my father   510
untainted by this guilt." Thus she spoke and with tears
and piteous groans she held forth the potent poisons and charms,
for the stars in the sky were already fading and Boötes had sunk
almost to touch the horizon. With what she was giving, she knew
she went herself, with her honor and her name and fame forever,
and he knew it, too, and reached out with his hand to hers—and took.
    And there in that moment, it happens, and she is beyond all guilt
and all sense of shame, which is useless in retrospect, for the past
cannot be changed. She accepts, as she must, the Furies' dominion
and with spell after spell she endows the body and mind of Aeson's   520

valiant son with magic powers and makes his shield
stronger and more resistant, and, muttering sevenfold charms,
gives his spear point an extra accuracy and sharpness.
Even as she does this, those distant bulls can feel
their fires cool and their strength ebbing. She gives to Jason
Discord's crested helmet, explaining to him its use:
"When you have plowed your furrows and the harvest springs up, fling this
helmet that Discord herself has held in her deadly hands
into the midst of the crop. The troop of soldiers will turn
530 on one another in rage and slaughter themselves, and my father
will cry aloud in dismay and wonder, and more than likely
look to me and blame me." But as she was saying these words,
her thoughts had already flown forward to the idea of the Minyae
at sea, the wind in their sails and their widening wake behind them,
departing without her. Her heart felt a sharp and terrible pang,
and she clutched at Jason's hand and begged him, "Do not forget me,
for I swear, after you've gone, I shall remember you always.
Only tell me what part of the sky I may look to, what star
to reckon by to direct my gaze toward your native land.
540 And you, meanwhile, may think, wherever you are, of me
and recall how, years ago, this was your sorry plight
in which you were not ashamed to be saved by the skill of a girl.
But what is this? Your eyes brim with tears at my words.
You have understood that my father in justifiable anger
will have me put to death, while for you a throne is waiting.
But see: I make no complaint. I am happy to give my life
and precious place in the light for the sake of saving yours."
To this, Jason replied as his heart prompted (or was it
because of her silent spell upon him that swayed his mind?):
550 "Do you think that I could accept your help and then turn away
to desert you or endure anywhere on earth a life
without you by my side? Better that you should abandon
me and my cause to your tyrant father, remove these spells,
and let me go to my death. What love of life and the world
could I, in such shame, maintain? How could I go home
unless my father, Aeson, embrace you in his arms
in affectionate welcome and thanks, and all Greece come to greet you
and watch in awe your approach with your glittering golden fleece?

Believe what I say, and be, if you will have me, my wife!
By the power of yours that sways the gods above and below,   560
by the stars whose course in the sky you can, by an act of will,
redirect, by this hour of trial and danger, I swear
that if ever I forget this night and these generous actions
you have performed for my sake — your flight from your father's scepter,
your home and parents — then let my triumph over the bulls
and the soldiers that spring from the earth be worthless and hateful to me;
let your magic turn against me in our own home;
let me be terrified; and let no one be near to help
such an ungrateful wretch as I should then be reckoned,
and if you then can think of more dreadful exactions, add them   570
for I shall have deserved the worst that you can do
as you turn away from me." And as he spoke, the Fury
who takes note of the pledges lovers exchange heard him
and noted it down for the future, in case his might prove false.

    Having said this, he stood there, as she did, with downcast eyes,
and then they looked at each other in joy and youth and love's
all but unbearably sweet delight, and they looked away
and could scarcely speak. But Medea composed herself to say
to Jason: "But I must tell you what perils will still await you
once you have vanquished those bulls. That fleece you want is guarded,   580
and you will need my help at the tree of Mars — that task
is daunting indeed! I wish my powers and Hecate's were equal
to what you need and so bravely assume we have." But words
can convey only so much. Better, by far, to show him.
She rouses the giant serpent and then summons up a phantom,
an image of Jason that makes it raise its fearsome head
and send forth a blood-chilling hiss. It coils around its tree trunk
and lunges and snaps and again snaps with its great jaws closing
on empty air. And Jason takes a step or two back
and looks in alarm at this horror. "What is this?" he asks,   590
baring his sword. She smiles and charms the snake back to sleep,
whereupon she speaks again. "This yet remains,
the last thing that my angry father has put in your way
the danger of which you must brave. If I could spare you this
and could see you climb that tree with its rough bark and twisted
branches to get to the fleece and trample beneath your feet

the coils of the sleeping monster, I would, at any cost —
even that of my own life — and I'd die happy."
Saying this, she fled back to the city where darkness,
600 its strength failing, was letting go its grip on the world.

         And now, beneath the roseate sky, the king goes forth
with his hopes high to look out at the river and see an expanse
of blue, empty again, and the ship gone or a dot
dwindling into the offing, but as he comes down to the shore
Echion confronts him, the Arcadian, Jason's herald,
to deliver his captain's message: "My leader is there already
on that field of Mars, awaiting your bronze-footed pyropnaeic
bulls to try his strength." And the king, taken aback,
asks, "What is this? That man is still here? Challenging me?"
610 But within him, he feels his heart sinking as hope shrivels
and his confidence bleeds away. Still, he maintains his manner
bellicose and brusque. "Then let the bulls be brought out
and we'll see if he can yoke them, withstand their fiery breath,
and use them to plow the field. And then, when the crop comes in,
we'll watch as the impudent Greek harvests what he has planted.
And if he should somehow survive, we'll look on with delight
at what happens when he encounters my daughter's serpent
that coils in the tree. How splendid to see those foreigners die
in sight of the fleece, and perhaps decorate with their gushing blood
620 that prize they failed to take." And at his command the bulls
are let loose onto the field, while his soldiers bring the monstrous
dragon's-teeth seeds, and servants drag out the huge plow.
And now onto the field with a throng of his men in escort
the valiant leader strides. They wish him well and withdraw
from the grim arena, while he remains for his ordeal,
planting his feet and ready for whatever may come. Imagine
a wheeling squadron of birds that swoop and ascend and one,
cut off and alone, remains in the burning Sahara's sands
or the snowy Riphaean crags of Scythia's windblown mountains.
630 And then the earth seemed to shudder and the sky was darkened to murk
in which there were sudden flashes of light, as from smoky fires,
when out of their stalls Aeëtes' bulls came lumbering forth
like twin forks of a bolt of lighting that Jove hurls down
on defenseless mankind, or like two winds that escape from their cave

and buffet together from different directions to tousle the trees.
That was how it seemed as the two fire-snorting bulls
emerged from their stalls to emit a whirlwind of flame and smoke,
holding their heads high as they breathed out conflagration.
In dismay the *Argo*'s crew shuddered, and even Idas,
brave as he was (he had scorned to be saved by the spells of a girl),   640
quailed at this apparition and his leader's dismal prospects,
and he looked to the Colchian maiden, hoping now for her help.
Abruptly, Jason charged to rush the bulls that were trotting
off to one side. He waved his helmet to catch their attention.
One of them, seeing him, turned and pawed the ground in anger,
delayed a moment, and then in sudden fury ran
at Jason—not more madly do waves rush onto the rocks
of cliffs from which they fall back into their broken spume.
It charges, and then again, with thunderous blasts of smoke
that envelop him, but Medea's charms protect him: the heat   650
does not seem to affect him but cools as it hits his shield,
imbued as it is with decoctions she has applied. Now Jason
seizes with his right hand the burning horns of the bull
and wrestles the beast and twists its head as he presses it downward
inch by laborious inch with all his strength. The bull
struggles too, against Jason and Medea's spells as well,
and tries to shake off the Greek, who stands there, motionless, twisting
and pressing still on the horns. The bull bellows in anger
but is sinking down and his snorts and roars are lower and fainter
as he falls at last to the turf having thus been bested.   660
Aeson's son then signals to his shipmates to bring him the bridle,
which he forces over the head of the bull, clamping its mouth
closed and holding it steady as it fights, but he fights back,
dragging and being dragged, until with his knee he fixes
the beast's quivering shoulders and forces upon it the huge
brazen yoke. Medea, meanwhile, mutters a spell
that tames the other bull, making it docile and guiding
its reluctant steps toward Jason. She casts upon it a cloud
and it sinks to the ground as if exhausted by its own weight
and rage, and Jason is now upon it, pressing it down.   670
Its roars are useless as Jason forces the yoke upon it
and he hitches the pair to the plow. With his knee he gets them up

and he uses his spear as a goad . . . Think of how Neptune brought
from a fissure deep in the earth the first horse, and Lapithes,
Apollo's son, put the first bridle on it and mounted
to ride in pride to Ossa's peak. So it is with Jason,
who now turns the sod as if on the Libyan plains or the fertile
farmlands along the Nile, scattering seeds by the handful
to sow on the fresh-tilled earth the crop of warfare's violence.

680   Three times from every furrow comes the sound of a martial trumpet
and the soil quivers and shakes as a phalanx sprouts to life
of men at arms springing up across the plain. The hero
withdraws for a time to rest and talk with his loyal companions
and to wait until the field should produce the troops' vanguard.
He looks and sees the furrows sprouting with helmet crests
and then the heads of soldiers. Among these he runs and cuts
with the sharp blade of his sword across their necks as the shoulders
heave into view. Like trees or bushes he prunes them back,
but behind and ahead there are more, corselets gleaming and arms

690   that he runs to hack at before they are free to brandish weapons.
But still they come, by the thousands, too many for any one man
without help. Think how great Hercules once in his battle
against the dreaded hydra needed the aid of Athena
and fire to use in the fight. Now Jason remembers Medea's
prescription and loosens the chin strap that fastens his charmed helmet.
He hesitates, preferring to win on his own, but the throng
is huge with men on all sides, shouting loudly, their banners
waving, their trumpets blaring. They see him now and advance,
flying at him, converging. Terrified, Jason flings

700   into their midst that helmet Medea has given him, looks,
and watches its hellish poison work as the spears turn away.
We know how Phrygians worship Cybele, mourning for Attis
and cutting themselves in their rite, or Bellona's devotees,
the eunuchs, slash themselves and one another with sharp
knives: in that way Medea's magic inflames and involves
this cohort that grows from the ground, and they turn their rage on
        themselves,
each of them thinking the brother soldier he kills is Jason
who is making himself as scarce as he can, as he watches in horror
this carnage. And so Aeëtes watches, astonished, appalled,

unable to intervene and recall them to reason. They kill
in a frenzy, disordered, savage, until there is not one left
and the earth, as if ashamed, opens to swallow her dead.

    In his blood-soaked armor, Jason hurries down to the river
to bathe, as Mars himself after his Getic warfare
entered the Hebrus, riding his car that scarred the water
with the hot sweat of the battle. Or think of a Cyclops, black
with grime from the hot hearth where the lightning bolts are forged
and to cleanse himself he plunges into Sicily's sea.
Now Jason returns to embrace his exulting comrades. The plan
is changed now: they no longer think to claim their prize
from the lying king. If he tried to give them the fleece, they'd refuse it,
preferring to take it by force and claim it as theirs. It's clear,
and they all know how things stand as in menace each side withdraws.

Book VIII

Back in her room at the palace, Medea, terrified, thinks
of what she has done to provoke her father's rage. Her fears
of the dark ocean, of exile, of a life among faraway strangers
are less than her fear of him. No country is distant enough
to which she can flee; no ship is too frail for her to trust
to take her away from his anger. In tears she bids farewell
to her old room, to her bed on which she tossed and turned
in lovesick misery's dreams. She flings herself down and murmurs
into her pillow her useless complaints: "Alas, O father,
if only I might leave with the tender embraces a daughter
wants from a parent. These tears I am shedding should count for something.
I weep, believe me, for you, whom I love as much as ever,
every bit as much as I love him whom I follow.
Perhaps the ship will go down and he and I will drown—
as I must suppose you are hoping. For my part, I pray your rule
over this land may be long and peaceful and that you be happy
and proud of your other children, from whom you take love and comfort."
Thus she spoke, but then she took from the funeral urns
in which she stored them the drugs and charms that one day Jason
would come to despise, and she put them in flasks she hid in her bosom,
or some she secreted in hollowed stones that were part of her necklace.
And last, she took up a sword and ran out, stung by the Furies'
lash, as desperate as Ino who fled with her son Palaemon
she forgot she held in her arms as she leapt from the cliff to the sea,
and Athamas, her husband, helplessly pounded the ground.
    And the hero, weighed down by his cares, came to the sacred grove

where he stood, concealed in shadows — but one who was watching could see
his face, which shone starlike in its youth and vigor. Just so
Endymion must have seemed as he lay stretched out in the moonlight
alone, his comrades dispersed, and the goddess looked down and saw him   30
and was irresistibly drawn by his all but unbearable beauty.
Jason was just as gorgeous, and for him a princess was waiting,
just as much in love. That girl one might well compare
to a dove terrified by the menacing shadow of some bird of prey,
a hawk from which it flees in its panic to light on some stranger's
shoulder. Jason held her and spoke to her comforting words:
"My dearest, your coming to me shall bring to me and my people
the greatest glory. In you, my voyage is well rewarded,
without any further prize of an animal's fleece. And yet,
because you have such wonderful powers, I ask of your goodness   40
of heart: help me even further and grant that I may fulfill
the hard command that was laid upon me and bring back home
that fabulous pelt. It's what my comrades have suffered and worked for."
And having said this, he seized her hand and kissed her palm.
     Breaking again into sobs, the girl managed to answer,
"For your sake, I leave my father's house and my family's wealth
and position. No more a princess, I give up these royal trappings
to follow my heart and you, and live as an exile. Keep me!
Be true to your pledge and to me, who are now all that I have.
The gods have heard our words, and these stars look down on us both   50
as I go with you to brave the seas and the perils of travel.
Only disaster can cleave us and send me back to my father
to face his angry gaze. This is my prayer to the gods
and to you, O stranger, to whom I entrust myself, absolutely."
     Saying this, she leads him with hurrying steps through a thick
and pathless wood, while he keeps close and his mind is filled
with pity and gratitude as he thinks of what she has done.
But then abruptly looming before him are billows of smoke
from the depths of which come gleams of an even more menacing light.
"What is it?" he asks. "The heavens seem to descend, and a star   60
of dreadful portent shines." She tells him that what he sees
is the awful eye of the dragon whose crested head emits,
whenever the monster is roused, those angry fitful flashes.
"I am its mistress, the only person it knows and fears,

and it calls out when it's hungry and asks me to give it food.
Do you want to approach it now when it sees you and it can fight?
Or will you let me help you again and close its eyes
in sleep, so that you can take that fleece it guards?" Once more,
Jason is overwhelmed and grateful beyond all words.

70   Medea raises her arms to the sky. In her hand she holds
her wand, and she recites her prayers to Father Sleep
in rhythmic incantations: "From all the four directions
I, the girl from Colchis, call upon you to come
and bid you descend in all your power upon the serpent.
You have helped me often before: with your horn I have gentled
the waves of the sea and the sky's storm clouds and lightning bolts.
Come now, reverend sir, to perform a more daunting task
and show that your might compares with that of your brother Death."
Then, to the snake, she speaks: "Your duty is now suspended.

80 You may turn away from the fleece you have faithfully guarded and rest.
As long as I'm here you have no reason for apprehension.
I will guard the treasure myself, and you may relax your vigil
and, after your long toils, sleep." The serpent, however, resists,
trying to stay awake to guard the golden pelt
and it keeps its shining eyes wide open. It shakes itself
and shudders but cannot fight the beguiling drowsy feeling
that seizes it as the Colchian girl asperses her drugs
and mutters her spells with words that weigh on its lowering lids,
as if it swam in the Styx and, sleepy, it feels its anger

90 guttering out like the flame of a lamp when the fuel is spent.
The crested head is nodding lower each time and its neck
sinks to touch the ground. Think of the Nile or the Po
when the ocean's tide is rising and the river water turns back
to flow upstream: just so was the dragon's will overwhelmed.
Medea, seeing it helpless, ran to it, weeping tears
for pity's sake and in shame for her own cruel behavior.
"Never once, in the darkest night," she exclaimed, "did I see you
asleep at your post like this, when I brought you the honey-cake supper
you nibbled out of my hand. You great, poor, hulking brute!

100 What can I say? This way, I didn't need to kill you.
But when you wake, you'll look at your tree and see that the fleece
is gone and slink away to spend your old age in another

and, I hope, a better grove. Forget about me. Forgive me.
And do not come hissing and spitting to follow where I have gone."
Then, to Jason, she says, "Hurry! Go get the fleece.
I've subdued the bulls and helped you kill the earthborn soldiers,
and here I've helped you again — I trust for the last time."
But Jason asks for advice. How should he climb the tree
to get to the fleece? Medea tells him to use the serpent
on the back of which he now can safely plant his feet.   110
The hero, the son of Aeson, son of Cretheus, trusts her
and using the snake as a ladder ascends to the heights of the ash
to the sheepskin's golden cloud that shines with the dazzle of Iris'
glowing robe as she flies through the sky to greet bright Phoebus.
Jason snatches his prize, the fruit, the reward of his labors,
and the tree at that moment, yielding the skin of Phrixus' ram,
the trophy now of his exploit, groans in pain and chagrin
as a gloom, deep and uncanny, descends to settle around it.
    The couple now emerge from the woods and head toward the river
and the landscape around them shines with the light of the fleece that Jason   120
drapes across his chest or wears on his neck like a scarf
or wraps over his shoulder as Hercules did with the pelt
of the Nemean lion. And now, from the river, the crew, looking up,
see the golden flash from the distance and send up a cheer, and the ship,
sharing the joy of its crew, moves on its own to approach
the nearer bank and greet its master, who now is running,
and he hurls the golden fleece before him onto the deck ·
as he and the breathless maiden bound aboard where he stands
for one moment triumphant, spear in hand, and exults.
    Her father, meanwhile, quivers in rage at the dismal report   130
that reaches his ear: the fall of his house and the flight of his daughter.
Her brother, Absyrtus, hearing the news, puts on his armor,
and the whole city assembles, running pell-mell to the river.
Even Aeëtes sprints as if he were still a youth
and is there in his battle dress, but what can he do? The water
is empty. The swift ship has sailed, is gone with the wind.
    Her mother looks out at the unrelenting blue of the water.
Her sister, the other women, the matrons and maidens, too,
hear her mother's voice keen as she wails on the air
to her daughter: "Stop! Come back! Turn the vessel around,   140

as surely you can, my darling, having such awesome powers.
Where do you go? Your kin are here, in your father's kingdom.
His wrath is not yet set against you. Why do you flee
to faraway Achaea, to live alone as a stranger?
Is that what you want? Is this the marriage you dreamed of? Is this
the day I hoped, myself, to live long enough to see?
If I were a bird, I could fly across the water . . . a bird,
with my claws I'd tear the face of that vile pirate and scream,
loud as an angry gull, to demand Medea's return.
150   She was engaged to be wed to Styrus, Albania's prince,
and not to you. Her parents never approved your suit.
Pelias never commanded that you should abduct from Colchis
one of their daughters. Keep the fleece; keep anything else
you've filched from our temples; but give her back. And yet my complaint
is not with you, for she is the one who willingly went,
whose passion consumes her and makes the girl behave as she does.
Ever since the oars of Thessaly's ship drew near,
she has not been herself, has taken no joy in our feasting, has never
smiled. Her color was gone, her voice was faint, and her eyes
160   had lost their luster, and I was a fool for not having noticed.
If only I had been smarter, I could have managed better:
Jason could have lived in the palace, a son-in-law,
and she wouldn't have fled. Or I could have gone myself to share
in their crimes and a life in sorry exile but still together,
in whatever city he lives in, this stranger with whom you've run off."
So her mother spoke, and adding their weeping words
were her sister and all her maidens in waiting, wailing, keening,
calling their mistress' name and a last farewell that the wind
shredded to tatters of meaningless vowels as it bore her away.
170   The *Argo* meanwhile was speeding homeward, running before
a brisk breeze, and the crew looked out and recognized landmarks
on shores they had passed before. Erginus, on watch on the poop,
addressed his chief with a warning: "Our troubles are not yet done.
We have the fleece we came for, but remember, O son of Aeson,
those rocks that crash together, that angry churning sea—
which came close to killing Tiphys. Can we risk another encounter?
Or ought we not change course and look for a different way home?
Not far from here are the seven mouths of the River Hister.

If we head upstream, we may discover an alternate passage
that will lead us back to the sea and avoid those Cyanean rocks.   180
The last time, we were lucky and took only minor damage.
Who knows if that luck will hold?" Thus Erginus spoke,
having no idea that the cliffs, through divine decree, no longer
crashed upon one another, a threat to shipping, but now
were anchored and fixed in position. The captain, Jason, replied:
"A point well taken, helmsman. I accept your wise suggestion.
Let us plot a course that, if longer, is probably safer.
We can show the flag to other peoples and kings and explore
remote parts of the world where nomads' wagon wheels
make tracks across spaces as wide and empty as any sea."   190
    By herself, abaft the helmsman, Medea, wrapped in a robe
that covered her face, clung to Minerva's gilded image,
sitting and weeping alone, ignored by all the Greek
princes, and filled with doubt about whether her union with Jason
would be what she'd hoped. As the ship passed by the Sarmatian coast,
the surf that breaks on the beaches muttered and sighed in pity
for the girl from Colchis, and there, at Thoas, Diana, enshrined,
wept for Medea's future and what it held in store.
No Scythian river or lake but mourned for her as she passed,
and the snows on the mountaintops melted and wept for the princess   200
whose realms were now diminished to the space she took up on that deck.
Even the Minyae, struck as they were by her sorry plight,
made no further complaint but agreed that she should come with them.
Her abject woe continued, and nothing Jason could do
or say had much effect: no dainties he brought her to eat
or stories he told her, describing the hills of Thessaly, pleased her.
    At length they reach the island in the mouth of the Hister, Peuce,
named for the nymph who used to live there. The river flows
rapidly past these nurslings, the channel islands, and Jason
anchors and here he confides in his comrades and tells them at last   210
that he is betrothed to Medea. With unfeigned joy they offer
congratulations, best wishes, and praise of her worth and beauty.
Jason raises altars to Pallas and also to Venus —
who take in them small pleasure, knowing full well what this marriage
portends. But Jason has no idea. He grins and looks handsome —
like Mars himself when he comes from the bloodstained Hebrus to Venus'

warmest welcome. Or think of Hercules, his labors
completed at last, arriving at heaven's banqueting hall
where Hebe, Juno's daughter, offers him cups of mead.
220   Venus puts on the best face she can manage, and Cupid
rouses Aeëtes' daughter from her funk of worry and gloom.
The Cytherean goddess offers the bride her saffron robe
and the double tiara with jewels—which will one day gleam on the brow
of another bride of Jason. Beauty Venus gives her,
a radiant face framed by her blonde hair gleaming and silky.
Here in Rome, at the Almo, the water washes away
the pain when Cybele's torches flare and processions wind
through the crowded streets, and no one imagines the bloody wounds
they have just exchanged in the goddess' cruel rites in the temple.
230   Such is the joy devotees seem to be able to take,
and it must have been something like that with Jason approaching the altar
to join his bride in prayer, with Pollux there to preside,
pouring the water and lighting the fire of ritual cleansing
as the couple turned in a solemn circle. But Mopsus looked
and noted how tongues of flame on the altar failed to ascend,
and the frankincense wasn't right and didn't sizzle: he saw
no long and happy marriage but a love that would soon burn out.
The gods seem unkindly disposed to this union, the prophet fears.
What will it do—to them, or, if they have them, their children?
240   But it's done, and they set about preparing the feast the abundant
woodland provides. They slaughter and dress the game and cook it,
the usual meat-in-a-pot or meat-on-a-stick that they eat
reclining on grassy mounds where once the god of the River
Hister had caught the nymph Peuce and bedded her there.
In the center, the place of honor, on a higher mound the bride
and groom have made their al fresco couch with the golden fleece
as its cover, Medea and Jason recline and preside together.

     But what comes now to disturb the nuptial party? A band
from Colchis in hot pursuit with Absyrtus, Medea's brother,
250   leading a quickly assembled flotilla with fighting men
whose spirits he has aroused with eloquent martial words:
"Men of Colchis, let us, who feel in our hearts both grief
and rage, make haste to pursue this kidnapper, rapist, and thief.

No Jove, no godlike hero, he's a common robber who flees
with Phrixus' sacred fleece and the girl, the princess — my sister.
Our houses are still standing, and the city's walls are unbreached.
We are not defeated but only gulled, and we must redeem
our honor, for which the return of the fleece and the girl will not
begin to suffice. What I want is more than that: to begin with,
the lives of the fifty sailors, and their ship sunk to the bottom!   260
And then we must punish Greece, whose walls and homes are my quarry.
Only then will I be content or able to face my father.
The rumor is that they plan to wed, and if that be true,
then I must attend, as her brother and representing our father,
whose gray hairs keep him at home. We will present ourselves
with banners flying and torches waving to do them the honor
the occasion deserves. A girl whose royal descent goes back
to the god of the sun should have a wedding the world remembers —
and I promise the Greeks, for as long as they live, will never forget it."

    Having thus spoken, Absyrtus encouraged his men and urged them   270
to make all haste as they boarded their ships and took their places
on the rowers' benches, while banners flapped in the wind and the helmsmen
set their course. With oars that had been, at that sunrise, trees
in leaf on the hillsides (for what can determined men not accomplish?),
they churned blue water white as they chased the flying ship
with its figurehead of Pallas as far as the mouth of the Hister
where Peuce's island lies in the river's mouth. When they see
the tip of the *Argo*'s mast and the topmost spars of its rigging,
raising a martial shout, they row all the harder, their prows
all homing in on the single vessel before them. Styrus,   280
with a grappling hook in hand, stands at the prow of his ship
where waves of rage batter his heart that his own betrothed
Medea is here. Others bring out their shields and spears,
feeling their satisfactory heft in their eager hands.
Still others are smearing pitch on the firebrands they will use
in the battle for which they are eager. They close on their target: the reach
is less and less, is within a javelin throw, and they yell
loudly and stamp their feet on the decks in menacing rumble.

    At this, the Minyae look out at a sea now bright with torches
and run at once to their ship, leaving Medea behind.   290

Jason leaps to the poop to grab his spear and helmet,
and the gleam of the torches shines on the burnished blade of his sword
and the boss of his shield. The crew are snatching up their weapons
and hurriedly falling in on the beach to meet the assault.
But Medea? What are you thinking? What have your crimes achieved?
You see how the men of Colchis in your brother's charge have followed
across the ocean's wide expanse that you thought would be safe.
But there's nowhere to hide and now either Jason, your lover, will die,
or else he will kill your brother—and either way you are ruined.

300 There is no escape. She knows this, and hides herself in that bower
of evil omen, resolved that, however events may turn out,
she will not endure the disgrace, but instead will end her life.

    Higher up, in heaven, Juno is not indifferent
as she looks down on her Minyae, outnumbered as they are
and, unless she helps them, doomed. She sees the Colchian fleet
advancing toward the beach and is moved to descend to earth
to open the cave where the winds and tempests dwell and to point
to the fleet that should be the target of their turbulent rage. They swoop
and converge on that one spot in the sea—through the rest of the world,

310 the water is glassy smooth and the air, dead calm, but here
enormous billows roll, the winds howl, and the ships
are pitching, yawing, and rolling as the weather drives them ashore.

    Styrus is hurled from his boat and winds up in the *Argo*'s rigging
where he hangs for a moment, then falls with a splash in the sea and sinks
but then bobs up as a great wave flings him onto the shingle.
Behind him, the Colchian vessels are bouncing about like corks,
their prows now pointing to heaven and now to the depths below,
to which some few descend. On the others, the glimpses of faces
the lightning flashes reveal are snapshots of abject terror

320 in a no-man's-land where the downward deluge encounters the upward
splashing of salty spume from the polyphloisboisterous sea.
Styrus, yet undaunted, rouses himself and calls
to his men to ignore or defy the gods and close in battle:
"The woman is mine! Betrothed! With a rich dowry paid.
Can she then go off that way with some Greek who has no respect
for the institution of marriage? Out of how many princely suitors
was I the one her father chose? Was his judgment worthless?

Or does Jason think he's better, or braver, or does she think so?
Without any help from her magic, I could have yoked those bulls
or slain those earthborn men with this sword I hold in my hand,   330
which Jason now will encounter. You'll see which of us two
will prove to be the better and stronger man in a fight
Medea will find worth watching. I'll cut off his goddamn head
and throw it into the water like bait for fish with the blood
still spilling out of the neck. I'll cut off his goddamn dick,
turn him into a eunuch, and give him better perfume
than a pretty-boy's myrrh — instead, he'll reek of pitch and sulfur.
All I need is a break from these waves, that they set me upright
on the beach, where I shall show that Aeëtes' faith in me,
when he chose me as son-in-law to the son of the Sun, was not   340
misplaced. Am I wrong? Am I crazy? Is Medea still working magic?
Did she conjure up this storm with her duppy-dust and her spells,
open the sky's sluice gates, and churn up the turbulent sea?
Is she saving Jason's bacon with mumbo-jumbo again?
To hell with that hoo-doo horseshit. She'll see. It won't work anymore.
Come on, men. Follow me. Our ships can ride out this squall.
A woman is making mischief, but I say, pay it no mind."
  He lunges forward. Behind him his comrades pull at their oars,
but the boat as it hits the beach is breaking up and it founders
and this way and that spills men and spars and floating oars.   350
He runs back into the water to help whomever he can
of the men who are calling out as they stagger and fall in the surf.
He shouts and hurries to help them get to their feet, but a wave
knocks him over. He's down, but he rises again, and another
mountainous wave hits, and he loses his footing, falls,
goes under, and this time does not come up. The slate with his claim
to the hand of the maiden of Colchis is thus at last washed clean.
  Absyrtus is stricken with grief at the terrible thing he has seen.
What can he do? With his ships he can seal off the mouth of the river,
and then, having trapped them, attack, hitting the Minyae hard.   360
He staggers away from the wreckage, formulating a plan
as he walks down the coast to the west to a double bend in the river
across from Peuce. The *Argo*, moored there, lies at anchor.
That's where he will besiege the Greeks. He will watch the water's

ving and wait for a break in the storm and a fighting chance.
at as he stares out at the Greeks and calculates the odds,
Juno stares down from heaven, contriving her own resolution.
    On their side, the Minyae, who see what a fix they are in, are asking
the obvious question of Jason: why should he risk the lives
370 of so many men of courage and honor, his friends and companions,
for the sake of a single girl, a foreign woman, a stranger?
Is this what they all deserve, having worked so hard and suffered,
having come all this way? Is he crazy? Or out of his mind with lust?
Or has he adopted some fanciful notions of chivalrous conduct
where a band of heroes is happy to fight for the joys of nookie?
Give the girl back. They'll go home and leave us in peace with the sheepskin.
And we can go back to Greece in honor. Don't let this fury
you've brought along be the cause of a war between Europe and Asia.
Mopsus has prophesied it could come to pass that our heirs
380 on both sides will fight this battle over again—a kidnapped
woman, the bloodshed of heroes, the burning and looting of cities.
    Jason groans in the pain of hearing his friends' complaint.
They have made a convincing case, and yet he has taken the vows
of matrimony. The prospects of married life and its fresh
pleasures are eloquent, too, and he wants to fight, to protect her
whom he knows he owes. But he owes his shipmates as well, and at last
he yields to their greater claim and agrees—they will leave her behind.
But he temporizes a little. They must wait for a break in the weather.
As long as this storm keeps raging, it's madness even to think
390 of putting to sea. And until that time, he requires of them
their silence. The girl must not know the cruel decision he's made.
    Medea nevertheless suspects. Uncertain of him,
unhappy, suspicious, involved in a marriage she does not trust,
she can read his face and the signs in the faces of all the crew.
She sees how they turn away as she passes. They cannot meet
her glance, and they frown, and they do not speak. She knows her husband
is about to be untrue and betray his vows and her,
but she will not be passive and merely allow it to happen. Instead,
she draws him aside and makes him listen to her as she asks:
400 "Do the brave Minyae discuss me? Do you talk behind my back?
Am I your wife or merely a captive on Pelias' ship?
Don't I deserve to take part in these counsels? Or am I some servant,

a handmaid, chattel, a part of your expedition's loot?
We have taken our vows and I trust them and you, as a man of honor.
As long as the voyage lasts, you cannot put me aside,
not before we have reached home port in Greece. Your comrades
have not sworn an oath as you have, and if they can think to abandon
an inconvenient woman, you have no such option.
But neither does any of them. You think those people from Colchis
will be content with me? They will want the fleece, the ship   410
on which we have fled together, and the lives of all the crew.
Is the crew afraid? Are you? Do you worry that you are outnumbered?
Have you lost all faith in my powers? And am I not worth the risk?
If those men you call your comrades had come with another captain
and reached my father's shores, do you think they'd still be alive?
It's only because of me that those ingrates are homeward bound,
and they're ready now to abandon their only hope! You listen
to cowards and fools, but also hear the advice I give you,
who helped you yoke the bulls and put the serpent to sleep.
I hate to think what would happen if my love for you and my powers   420
were not so great as they are! But you know the answer to that.
So what are you planning? What commands will you issue to them and me?
Speak up! Or are you too ashamed to admit what you and your crew
have already agreed? Oh, brave and noble Jason!
Do I get down on my knees as a suppliant, begging for mercy?
This is beyond the worst that my father could ever imagine
as penance for all my crimes, to be a slave and despised . . ."
        She breaks off. Jason is silent. She storms away in a fury,
crying aloud like a frenzied Boeotian bacchant in the hills
as she flees into the trees. Maddened with anger and grief,   430
she runs as if to elude the depredation of ogres,
the threat of charging bulls, and the venom of nightmare monsters.
She'd thought she'd live to see the mountains of Greece, but no,
not even that. In disgrace she'll be left behind, betrayed.
She spends the day in weeping, muttering imprecations,
shouting defiant complaints, howling like wolves or lions
or lowing like cows whose heifers have been led away to the slaughter.
To see or hear her, you'd never suppose that this was a princess,
noble, powerful, proud, the royal Sun's granddaughter.
        Jason searches her out, ashamed of himself and his men,   440

but mindful of what he's agreed to. Still, he says what he can,
soothing her grief as he holds her and feeling as much as hearing
her body-racking sobs: "Do you think this was my idea?"

And here it breaks off. Valerius Flaccus dies, and his poem
is incomplete. But the story goes on, as stories do
in other poets' words in the minds of men, and we know
what happens next: Medea has betrayed her father and king
and has seen the death of her suitor. She cannot go back. Her lot
she has cast with Jason, this slender reed, for whom love alone
450   seems not to be enough. What else can she count on but guilt,
a stronger bond that the two people who share it can never
evade or deny? (And this is the worst of all possible deeds,
the worst crime she can imagine — but her future holds even worse.)
She proposes a plan to her husband: what he must do is to send
a herald across to Absyrtus with a message from her to announce
that, having been abducted, she wants to come home and will bring
the fleece, if her brother will come to meet her alone on Artemis'
island, just downstream from Peuce. "And offer him gifts,
splendid trophies to make him think that he is the victor
460   and let him be proud and exult. I've no doubt that he will come,
and you can emerge from hiding, surprise him, and easily kill him."
It's a way out, and he takes it, persuaded or hypnotized.
At any rate, he agrees, and forthwith Echion goes
to deliver the invitation along with Hypsipyle's robe
that Dionysus gave to Thoas, his son, who in turn
gave it to her, a sacred garment the Graces had made.
Absyrtus agrees to appear, and later that night wades ashore
on the beach of the sacred island. Medea, waiting, waves
and sees him running toward her, and then, from behind him, Jason
470   approaching, his sword upraised. And now to the crime of treason
fratricide is added, but this deed in its foulness will join
her with Jason forever, or so she thinks, as she notes
a starlight glint on the blade as it falls, and her brother falls
and bleeds and dies. Medea turns away then in horror
and also disgust, for Jason — Apollonius says this —
cuts off the arms and legs of the corpse and dips his hands

three times in the gouts of blood that he licks three times, and he spits,
as murderers used to do to expiate their crimes.
  Better than love? Such shackles are certainly stronger. The pair
are joined in that moment forever. They go back to Greece in the *Argo*,   480
and Mopsus is right: their marriage is neither long nor happy,
as Euripides makes clear, and Seneca also. Jason,
having broken his solemn vow, winds up a homeless outcast
like Oedipus wandering this way and that, from city to city,
and hated by men. At last he comes to the hull of the *Argo*
on Corinth's beach, by now an undistinguished hulk,
and he thinks to hang himself from what's left of the prow, when the ship,
as if to spare him this last indignity, topples over
and the weight of its wood crushes the man who was once its master.
  But the rest of them are with us still, those glints of starlight   490
Medea saw on the blade of her husband's sword. Look up
and observe in the sky the zodiacal signs that journey forever:
the ram is Phrixus' ram; the bull is Aeëtes' bull;
the lion is Rhea's lion that Cyzicus killed to bring on
his curse; the goat is a symbol of the lusty doings at Lemnos;
the twins are Castor and Pollux; and the archer is Hercules,
their shipmate. The other figures are parts of the story as well:
Aquarius, the Aegina water bearer; Libra,
King Alcinous' scales; and even Pisces, the fish,
that in some versions swallows Jason as if he were Jonah   500
and spits him back up, alive. In the old Egyptian system,
there's a serpent in Scorpio's house — the snake that guarded the fleece —
and a scarab instead of the Crab, a symbol of regeneration
of the kind Medea promised Pelias' daughters she'd conjure
for their agèd, enfeebled father, whom they cut into pieces and boil.
Which leaves us only Virgo, the Princess Medea herself.
What happens to her is an odd reversal: the gods, in their grief,
or perhaps remorse for having abused her so, relent.
She goes back in the end to Colchis, to kill her uncle Perses,
that traitor and usurper; she restores her father Aeëtes   510
to the throne he'd lost; and she never dies but dwells and reigns
in Elysian Fields forever with her husband, the great Achilles.

Printed in the United States
47138LVS00006B/28-78